W9-CAH-323

ALL OF TUSCANY

FLORENCE - SIENA - PISA - GROSSETO - AREZZO - PISTOIA - LUCCA - MASSA - LIVORNO

ABBEY OF SAN GALGANO - ABETONE - BAGNI DI LUCCA - BARGA - BORGO A MOZZANO - CARRARA - CASTIGLIONE DELLA PESCAIA - CERTOSA DI PISA - CHIANCIANO - COLLE DI VAL D'ELSA - COLLODI - CORTONA - FIESOLE - FOLLONICA - FORTE DEI MARMI - ISOLA D'ELBA - ISOLA DEL GIGLIO - LA VERNA - MASSA MARITTIMA - MONTALCINO - MONTECATINI TERME - MONTENERO - MONTEPULCIANO - MONTERIGGIONI - ORBETELLO - PIENZA - PITIGLIANO - POPPI - POPULONIA - PORTO ERCOLE - PORTO SANTO STEFANO - PRATO - PUNTA ALA - ROSELLE - SAN GIMIGNANO - SAN MINIATO - SAN PIERO A GRADO - SATURNIA - SORANO - TALAMONE - TORRE DEL LAGO - VETULONIA - VIAREGGIO - VINCI - VOLTERRA

THE ETRUSCANS IN THE MAREMMA - THE CHIANTI - THE MAREMMA - MEDICI VILLAS - THE AMIATA

BONECHI

INTRODUCTORY NOTE

Tuscany is one of the richest regions in Italy with a view to history, monuments, works of art, and magnificent landscapes. We hope that the many pictures in our presentation and the accurate exhaustive text which accompanies them will give you an idea of these many facets.
Our ideal itinerary begins in Florence and then touches on Pistoia, Lucca, Massa, and Pisa, in that order, to continue with Livorno, Grosseto, Siena and Arezzo. Each principal city is followed by information on the smaller towns and villages, alternating with general comments on areas of particular interest to the tourist, such as the Maremma, the sites of the Etruscan civilization, Mount Amiata and the valley of the Chianti.

© Copyright
CASA EDITRICE BONECHI,
Via Cairoli 18/b
50131 Florence - Italy
Telex 571323 CEB

All rights reserved.
No part of this work may be reproduced or utilized without the prior written permission of the publisher.

Printed in the EEC
by the Centro Stampa Editoriale Bonechi

Editing: Maurizio Martinelli
Layout: Stefano Grisieti
English translation: Erika Pauli (Studio Comunicare, *Firenze*)
The photographs are the property of the Archives of the
Casa Editrice Bonechi and were taken by:
Gaetano Barone, Carlo Cantini, Luciano Casadei,
Leonardo Castellucci, Renzo Cecconi, CISCU Lucca,
Roberto Germogli, Stefano Giusti, Foto Grassi, Stefano
Grisieti, Italfotogieffe, Nicolò Orsi Battaglini, Pisa Story,
Andrea Pistolesi, Pubbli Aer Foto, Antonio Quattrone,
Alessandro Saragosa, Soprintendenza Archeologica per la
Toscana, Soprintendenza ai Monumenti di Firenze, Fabrizio
Tempesti, Marzio Toninelli, Aldo Umicini.

HISTORY

There is no doubt that in prehistoric times many areas in Tuscany were already inhabited, as witnessed by interesting finds in the territories of Arezzo, of Siena (Paleolithic) and in the rest of the region (Neolithic and age of metals). Finds from the long period of the bronze age, dating back to 1500 B.C., are already considered historical and include pottery, tools and weapons in stone, bone and metal. The Villanovan culture belongs to the Iron Age (9th-8th cent. B.C.) and is the prelude to the birth here of the great Etruscan civilization. In the 7th and 6th centuries the Etruscans went beyond the current borders of the region and occupied parts of Latium, Campania, Umbria, the valley of the Po and Corsica. During these centuries the Etruscans controlled a large portion of the peninsula and brought a high degree of civilization and progress to the areas they ruled. But in the 5th-4th centuries they were attacked by other peoples who had in the meantime been growing in power and culture. They gave way to the Greek and Carthaginian supremacy of the seas and that of the Celts and Romans on land and were in the end forced to stipulate peace treaties with the Romans, who were the new political force on the peninsula. The policy adopted by the Romans in Etruria was particularly intelligent and permitted the conquered Etruscan cities to retain a partial autonomy. They also sponsored numerous public works (among other they connected Etruria to the most important communication routes). Even so the region slowly and inexorably declined as the population continued to diminish. At the beginning of the Imperial age Tuscany became the VII region of the Roman Empire. In the 3rd century A.D., under the reign of Diocletian, Etruria, now known as Tuscia, was joined to Umbria. In the early Middle Ages Tuscia's decline, which was to continue under Lombard rule, set in. Once - flourishing centers such as Lucca, Pisa, Arezzo and Florence became ever less important. The arrival of the Franks (A.D. 774) marked a turn for the better. The region was divided into feuds and with feudalism the abandoned cities of Tuscia slowly came back to life. The Crusades meant new life for one city in particular - Pisa. A city on the sea, and therefore favored in trade, Pisa was the center where the various Tuscan feudataries met before setting sail for the East from the port of Pisa. In the meanwhile other Tuscan cities, in particular Florence (in the field of textiles) and Siena (for banking activities), began to acquire power. With the passage from the feudal period to that of the communes, Tuscia, by now called Toscana, began a long period marked by struggles between rival cities: these were the years of the Guelphs and the Ghibellines, of antagonism between Florence and Pisa, between Siena and Florence. The city which gradually succeeded in coming to the fore was Florence and by the early 14th century it was the most powerful city in the region. Even proud Pisa was forced to surrender to this most powerful of Tuscan cities in 1406. With free access to the sea, Florence was now politically and economically independent. The only cities which still resisted were the small but solid republics of Siena and Lucca. During the 15th century, the Medici, rich and intelligent Florentine bankers, took over the power and transformed the communal status of Florence into a principality, and in the second half of the 16th century, under Cosimo I de' Medici, it officially became the Grand Duchy of Tuscany, of which Siena and Lucca, who had also been forced to surrender, now made part. This was the beginning of a long period of great success for the region. The opulence of Florence, which was also reflected in the other Tuscan cities, permitted the region to live the greatest period in its history. During the periods of Humanism and the Renaissance, Florence and Tuscany became the cradle of international culture. In 1737 the last of the Medici Grand Dukes, Gian-gastone, ceded the sceptre of the Grand Duchy to the Lorraine dynasty, who continued to govern with intelligence and broadmindedness. As a result of great changes in the international scene at the end of the 18th century and of Napoleon's rise to power, the Grand Duchy of Tuscany was annexed to the French Empire until the dictator's fall. Then came the Risorgimento and the revolutionary movements for the Union of Italy, and in 1866 Tuscany was annexed to the new Kingdom of Italy. Five years later Florence became the capital of the new nation and remained such until 1870. At the beginning of the 20th century the population began to increase and the towns started to develop; these were the years tormented by the «social question»: the vindications of the workers, the birth of fascism. In World War II, Tuscany took an active part in the struggle for liberation and when the war was over initiated a reconstruction activity which led to industrialization.

FLORENCE

The river Arno cuts its way through the broad plain on which Florence lies, surrounded by the out-hills of the Tusco-Emilian Apennines. Already occupied in prehistoric times, as early as the 8th century B.C. an Italic peoples with a Villanovan culture settled in the area between the Arno and Mugnone rivers, but little is known of these remote times. In 59 B.C. the Roman city was founded with the square ground plan of the *castrum*. The *decumanus maximus* was laid out along what are now the Via del Corso, the Via degli Speziali and the Via Strozzi, while the ancient *cardo* corresponds to the line between Piazza San Giovanni, the Via Roma and the Via Calimala. With the arrival of the barbarians, Florence was first besieged by the Ostrogoths (405) of Radagaisus, who plundered the surrounding countryside, although Florence managed to resist and Stilicho's troops inflicted an overwhelming defeat on the enemy. Next came the Byzantines, who occupied Florence in 539, and the Goths who took over the city in 541. Under Lombard domination (570) it managed to safeguard its autonomy, while under the Franks the number of inhabitants diminished and the city lost most of its territory. Around the year thousand, things began to change for the better and the "lily" city's rise continued for various centuries in spite of numerous controversies, wars and internecine struggles. New walls surrounded the city, new civic and religious buildings went up, and at the same time the arts, literature, and trade continued to prosper. In 1183 the city became a free commune, even though it had already actually availed itself of this freedom for many years. The first clashes between the two factions, Guelph and Ghibelline, date to those years. The former were followers of the Pope, the latter of the Emperor. The ensuing struggles were to lacerate the civic fabric of the city up to 1268. Despite the unstable social and political situation, this period witnessed an upsurge in the arts and in literature. This was the time of Dante and the «*dolce stil novo*», of Giotto and Arnolfo di Cambio. In the 15th century the city's rise continued. Florence was a trading city but also the new cradle for Italian and eventually European culture. Many powerful families (the Pitti, Frescobaldi, Strozzi, Albizi) vied for supremacy in the city. One above all soon came to the fore, a powerful family of bankers - the Medici - and beginning with the founder Cosimo I, later known as the Elder, they were to govern up to the first half of the 18th century, transforming Florence into a beacon during the period of Humanism and the

Above: a view of the rooftops with the Baptistery, the Duomo and Giotto's Campanile; right: the facade of the Duomo flanked by Giotto's Campanile.

Renaissance. Great personalities such as Leonardo da Vinci and Michelangelo characterized the period and Florentine prestige reached its zenith.

In 1737 the Medicis gave way to the house of Lorraine and the government continued along the lines of a moderate liberalism even if at that point the great period of Florentine culture was on the wane. In 1860, during the Risorgimento, Tuscany was annexed to the Realm of Italy with a plebiscite. For a brief period Florence then became the capital of the new nation.

DUOMO

The Duomo or Cathedral of Florence, dedicated to Santa Maria del Fiore, is the fruit of the commitment of a large number of artists such as Arnolfo di Cambio, Giotto, Andrea Pisano and Brunelleschi who worked on it over a period of centuries, beginning in 1296. Arnolfo's **facade** was torn down in 1587 and designs for a new one abounded. Not until 1871 were the plans by De Fabris approved and they were then carried out in 1887. Above the three portals with *Stories from the Life of the Virgin* are three lunettes with, left to right, *Charity*,

the *Madonna with the Patrons of the City*, and *Faith*. The gable of the main entrance has a *Madonna in Glory*. Statues of the *Apostles* and of the *Virgin* form the frieze between the rose windows at the side and the one in the center. The tympanum with a bas-relief of *God the Father* is set above a row of busts of artists. In the interior there is a strong feeling for space, both vertical and horizontal, in keeping with the dictates of Italian Gothic architecture. The aisles flow into the area of the high altar around which the three apses or tribunes, each divided into five rooms, radiate. Under the stained glass designed by Ghiberti and Paolo Uccello's *Clock* (1443), the **interior facade** bears the 14th-century lunette with the *Coronation of the Virgin* by Gaddo Gaddi, and the *tomb of Antonio d'Orso*, by Tino di Camaino, around 1321. The **left aisle** is only apparently unadorned for it contains various masterpieces of art: at the beginning is the aedicule with a statue of *Joshua*, by Ciuffagni, Donatello and Nanni di Bartolo, and the neighboring *aedicule of S. Zanobius* painted at the end of the 14th century by Vanni del Biondo. Between Benedetto da Maiano's *bust of A. Squarcialupi* and

Left, above: the interior of the Duomo of Florence; below: a portion of the old cathedral of
Florence, Santa Reparata, which can be seen under the Duomo; above: the dome designed and
built by Brunelleschi.

equestrian monuments, detached frescoes of *Giovanni
Acuto* (John Hawkwood) and *Niccolò da Tolentino*.
In front of the arch of the fourth bay, under the *stained
glass window* designed by Agnolo Gaddi, are the panels
with *SS. Cosmas and Damian* (by Bicci di Lorenzo, 15th
cent.) and *Dante* (by Domenico di Michelino, 1465).
Two marble aedicules flank the door of the **Sacrestia
Nuova** (New Sacristy) with a lunette in glazed terracotta
by Luca della Robbia. On the opposite side, beyond the
high altar - a 16th-century work by Baccio Bandinelli -
there is, in mirror image, the door of the **Sacrestia Vecchia** (Old Sacristy) with Luca della Robbia's other lunette of the *Ascension*. The right tribune contains a
Giottesque fresco with the *Madonna* and a *St. Philip* by
Bandini. Beyond this in the south aisle is a painting of
St. Bartholomew Enthroned by Franchi (15th cent.) and
the aedicule with a *Prophet* by Nanni di Banco (1408),
set between a *roundel* of Giotto (by Benedetto da
Maiano, 1490) and a bust of Brunelleschi (by Buggiano,
1446). Here a modern staircase descends to the pre-
existant church of Santa Reparata.

At the time **Santa Reparata** was situated where the front
part of the cathedral now stands. The church had been
built in the 4th-5th centuries on the ruins of a Roman
domus, and it was tripartite with columns and a single
apse. At the time of the Byzantine wars the church was
destroyed and then rebuilt between the 8th and 9th centuries. Although the perimeter remained basically the
same, two side chapels were added to the structure and
the columns were replaced by piers with pilaster strips.
Between the year 1000 and 1100 a crypt with a raised
choir was created in the area of the apse, which was
flanked by two bell towers outside.
The great **dome** of the Cathedral of S. Maria del Fiore,
which Brunelleschi had conceived as bare, was however
painted by Giorgio Vasari and Zuccari between 1572
and 1579. Scenes from the *Last Judgement* are set in
three concentric bands with the *Prophets* at the top of
the vault in a *trompe l'œil* lantern with a railing. A pas-
sageway let into the thickness of the dome leads to the
frescoes and from the terrace above the high altar continues up to the lantern at the top of the cathedral.

Above, left: the Baptistery of San Giovanni; right: the mosaics on the interior of the octagonal dome; facing page: the Gates of Paradise, by Ghiberti, as they were before the onset of atmospheric degradation.

BAPTISTERY

The Florentine Baptistery seems originally to have been built around the 4th-5th century and was rebuilt as it is today, with its **exterior** facing of white and green marble, in 1293.

Each side is divided into three areas by pilaster strips which support a trabeation below and round arches with windows above.

The three sets of bronze doors are particularly important. The **South Doors**, which are the oldest and which are decorated with scenes from the *Life of St. John the Baptist* and the *Allegories of the Theologian and Cardinal Virtues*, are by Andrea Pisano (1130-1336). The **North Doors** with *Stories from the New Testament, Evangelists* and *Doctors of the Church* are by Lorenzo Ghiberti (1403-1424), with the help of Donatello, Bernardo Ciuffagni, Paolo Uccello and Bernardo Cennini. And lastly the **East Doors** known as the «*Gates of Paradise*» with ten panels (now replaced by copies) which represent *Stories from the Old Testament*. The work of Lorenzo Ghiberti, this ensemble is one of the greatest masterpieces of 15th-century sculpture. The **interior** has an inlaid pavement with decorative motifs of eastern derivation. On the walls from left to right: a Roman *sarcophagus*, the *sarcophagus of Bishop Ranieri* and the *tomb of Baldassare Coscia, the Antipope John XIII* (1427), designed by Michelozzo and Donatello. The tribune in the apse has Byzantine style *mosaics* on the vault done around 1225 by Fra Jacopo. Other mosaics cover the entire **cupola** at which Florentine artists, possibly aided by Venetian craftsmen, worked between the 13th and the 14th centuries. These artists included Cimabue, Coppo di Marcovaldo and Gaddo Gaddi. The tondo above the apse represents *Christ* surrounded by scenes of the *Last Judgement*. The opposite side contains *Stories of the Baptist*, scenes from the *Life of Christ*, and from the *Life of Joseph and Mary* as well as *Stories from Genesis*. The *Angelic Hierarchies* are represented around the lantern.

GIOTTO'S CAMPANILE

The Cathedral bell tower was begun in 1334 by Giotto, who as *capomastro* was overseer for the construction of the Duomo.

Up to his death in 1337, he built the bottom part of the campanile comprised of two closed stages decorated with hexagonal and rhomboid *reliefs*, by Andrea Pisano, Luca della Robbia, Alberto Arnoldi and workshop. The relief panels on the lower band, now replaced by casts, represent the *Life of Man* with *Genesis* and *Arts and Industries* executed by Andrea Pisano and Luca della Robbia to Giotto's designs.

The two upper stages were carried to completion by Andrea Pisano, who took Giotto's place at the time. He created a series of sixteen niches between the pilaster

Left: Giotto's Campanile; above: choir stall by Luca della Robbia. Facing page: Michelangelo's Deposition. Last two both in the Museo dell'Opera del Duomo.

strips which contained statues of the *Prophets*, *Sibyls* and the *Baptist*, surmounted by an equal number of false niches. Between 1350 and 1359 Francesco Talenti finished the campanile, adding two levels with the two gabled two-light windows with their lovely twisted columns and the stage with the single three-light opening. On the top, over 81 meters high, he created the large terrace supported by small arches and with an openwork balustrade.

MUSEO DELL'OPERA DEL DUOMO
Inside are numerous pieces of Romanesque sculpture, statues and architectural fragments from the ancient facade of the Duomo and the Baptistery. Some of the statues to be noted on the ground floor include *Boniface VIII in the Act of Blessing*, a *Madonna and Child*, and the *Madonna of the Nativity* by Arnolfo di Cambio, and the famous *St. Luke* by Nanni di Banco. The museum also contains the *Magdalen*, an intense and vibrant wooden statue by Donatello. On the first floor are the two *choir lofts*, one by Donatello and the other by Luca della Robbia, and various statues once set on Giotto's campanile. In the room at the right is the fine *altar frontal of St. John the Baptist*, a large monument on which Michelozzo, Verrocchio, Antonio del Pollaiolo and Bernardo Cennini collaborated. On either side are the statues of the *Virgin Annunciate* and the *Angel Gabriel* by Jacopo della Quercia. In the room on the left are the original *relief panels* from Giotto's bell tower, made for the two tiers of decorations: they are by Andrea Pisano, Alberto Arnoldi and Luca della Robbia. Other examples of painting and sculpture include a noteworthy diptych with scenes from the *Life of Christ and the Madonna*, of Byzantine school dating to the late 13th century, and Michelangelo's *Deposition*.

Above: the cubical building with the Church of Orsanmichele on the ground floor; left: Orcagna's Tabernacle with the Madonna and Child by Daddi, inside the same church.

CHURCH OF ORSANMICHELE

The structure was once a loggia used as a communal granary which later became an oratory. Built by Arnolfo di Cambio in 1290, it was transformed between 1337 and 1404.

A series of tabernacles and statues runs along the walls of the exterior of building. They are by Ghiberti, Donatello, Michelozzo, Andrea del Verrocchio, Giambologna, Nanni di Banco, including Donatello's famous *St. George* (1416) (bronze copy of the marble original now in the Bargello Museum). **Inside** is a series of frescoes and panels dedicated to the *Patron Saints* (14th-16th cent.). But the masterpiece is the magnificent *Tabernacle* by Orcagna (1355-59) in international Gothic style. The *panel* is by Bernardo Daddi.

The Piazza della Signoria with the Palazzo Vecchio and, on the right, the Loggia dei Lanzi.

PIAZZA DELLA SIGNORIA

This is one of the loveliest piazzas in Italy, scenographically arranged over a vast square area. The piazza took shape and was later enlarged between the 13th and 14th centuries thanks to the demolition of the houses of various Florentine Ghibelline families including the Uberti and the Foraboschi. The imposing complex of the **Palazzo Vecchio** towers over the piazza on the north side. To the right of the façade of the Palazzo Vecchio is the lovely **Loggia dei Lanzi**, a late Gothic structure by Simone Talenti (1376-82), enlivened by a row of important statues including Cellini's famous **Perseus** (1554) and Giambologna's **Hercules and the Centaur**. To the left of the palace is the lively **Fountain of Neptune**, or Fontana di Piazza, by Bartolomeo Ammannati (1563-75) and, to one side, the **Equestrian Monument of Cosimo I** (1594) by Giambologna. The square is framed by a sombre row of ancient palaces.

FONTANA DEL BIANCONE
(THE NEPTUNE FOUNTAIN)

This extremely theatrical sculptural group was executed between 1563 and 1575; the powerful figure of *Neptune* looms up in the center of the Fountain, one of Ammannati's less felicitous creations (the artist may have been inspired by a drawing of Leonardo's). Much more successful are the bronze statues which represent *River Allegories* of satyrs and nymphs, by Ammannati and some of his young collaborators including Giambologna.

EQUESTRIAN STATUE
OF COSIMO I DE' MEDICI

The monument stands on the left of the Palazzo Vecchio. The work is restrained and noble with the proud pose of the *condottiero* and the imposing muscles of the horse, which Giambologna, as a mature artist, was capable of creating (1594). The bas-reliefs of the pedestal show the *Entry of Cosimo into Siena, Pio V Giving Cosimo the Insignia of the Grand Duke, The Tuscan Senate Giving Cosimo the Title of Grand Duke.*

Left: the Fountain of Neptune known as Biancone; below: the Loggia dei Lanzi.

Above: the interior of the Loggia dei Lanzi; right: Cellini's famous Perseus.

LOGGIA DEI LANZI

Built by Benci di Cione and Simone Talenti between 1376 and 1391, it consists of large round arches on compound piers, although there is also an emphasis on horizontal rhythms. Of late Gothic taste, the Loggia is very elegant. The fine reliefs above the piers are allegories of the *Virtues*, after designs by Agnolo Gaddi. On either side of the stairs lions flank the access: one is an example of classic art, the other is by Flaminio Vacca (1600). Various outstanding examples of statuary are sheltered **inside** the Loggia: in front, to the left, is Cellini's famous *Perseus* (1553), at the center are *Hercules and the Centaur*, by Giambologna (1559), *Ajax with the Body of Patrocles*, a restored piece of Hellenistic sculpture, and the *Rape of Polyxena* by Pio Fedi (1886). Six antique Roman statues of matrons are set against the back wall.

Above, left: the facade of Palazzo Vecchio; below: the Studiolo of Francesco I; above: the interior of the Salone dei Cinquecento. Facing page, above: the Sala dei Gigli and, below, the Siege of Florence painted in the Hall of Clement VII.

PALAZZO VECCHIO

Begun in 1294 as a palace-fortress for the residence of the Priors, Arnolfo di Cambio conceived of the building as a large block crowned by crenellations. The characteristic feature is the powerful thrust of the **Tower** which rises up above the palace and which echoes the terminal part. A row of statues is set in front of the building, including a copy of Michelangelo's *David* and *Hercules and Cacus* (1534) by Baccio Bandinelli. On the left of the observer is the large *Fountain of Neptune*. Immediately **inside** is the first **Cortile** or courtyard rebuilt by Michelozzo. Two spacious flights of stairs (by Vasari) lead on each side to the **Salone dei Cinquecento,** an enormous hall built by il Cronaca and decorated by a host of painters chosen by Vasari. Michelangelo's sculpture of *Victory* is on the longer wall to the right. A door at the far right of the entrance leads to the **Studiolo of Francesco I,** the **Tesoretto of Cosimo I** (by Vasari), the **Salone dei Duecento** (1441) by Giuliano and Benedetto da Maiano, and the **State Apartments** which include many rooms with a wealth of paintings and frescoes. A staircase to the second floor leads to the **Quartiere degli Elementi,** by Battista del Tasso and to the **Apartment of Eleonora of Toledo** by Vasari.

Facing page: the courtyard of the Uffizi; above: the Gallery inside the museum.

UFFIZI

The gallery of the Uffizi is the most famous picture gallery in Italy and one of the best known in the world. It furnishes a complete panorama of the various schools of Florentine painting, represented by important works and authentic masterpieces. The Uffizi was commissioned from Giorgio Vasari by the Medicis as administrative and judicial offices (thence the name). Begun in 1560 and finished twenty years later, the two wings with a loggiato at the bottom are connected by a third wing with arches along the Arno. The visit to the Gallery begins on the second floor. This great museum did not become public patrimony until 1737, a gift of Anna Maria Ludovica de' Medici, the last of this prestigious family. The gallery consists of 45 rooms divided into sections.

Room 1 (The Archaeological Room). The room contains a *torso* in green basalt, Roman copy of a Doryphoros by Polykleitos.

Room 2 (Tuscan painting of the 13th century and Giotto). This room contains some of the greatest works of this period such as the *Santa Trinita Madonna* by Cimabue (1285), the *Rucellai Madonna (Madonna Enthroned with Six Angels)* (1285) by the Sienese painter Duccio da Buoninsegna, and Giotto's *Ognissanti Madonna (Madonna and Child Enthroned with Angels and Saints)* (1310).

Room 3 (Sienese painting of the 14th century). On exhibition are works by Pietro and Ambrogio Lorenzetti, as well as the splendid *Annunciation with Saints* (1333) by Simone Martini, a large triptych focussed on the intimate and touching dialogue between Gabriel and the Virgin; the figures of *Saints Ansano and Giulitta*, at the sides, are by Lippo Memmi, Simone Martini's brother-in-law.

Room 4 (Florentine painting of the 14th century). Many works by the most prestigious Florentine masters are collected here: Taddeo Gaddi, Bernardo Daddi, Giottino, Giovanni da Milano.

Room 5-6 (International Gothic). Particularly striking in this room are the brilliantly colored *Adoration of the Magi* (1425) by Gentile da Fabriano and Lorenzo Monaco's exuberant triptych of the *Coronation of the Virgin* (1413).

Room 7 (Early Renaissance Florentine painting). The outstanding paintings in this room include the *Madonna and Child with St. Anne* (1420-24) by Masaccio and terminated by Masolino da Panicale; the *Battle of San Romano* (1456) by Paolo Uccello, and the *Portraits of Federico da Montefeltro and his wife Batista Sforza* (1465), two splendid profiles by Piero della Francesca.

Room 8 (Florentine painting of the 15th century). Also known as the Filippo Lippi room because so many of the works of this great master are on exhibit here, including the *Adoration of the Child with Saints*, the *Coronation of the Virgin*, the *Madonna and Child with an Angel*. The room also contains interesting works by Alessio Baldovinetti such as the *Madonna and Child with Saints* and the *Annunciation*. Early works by Botticelli such as the *Madonna of the Rose Garden*, and the *Madonna Enthroned and Saints* by Lorenzo di Pietro called Vecchietta.

Room 9 (Florentine painting of the 15th century, known also as the Pollaiolo room). This room contains numerous works by the brothers Antonio and Piero del Pollaiolo. By Antonio let us recall the famous *Portrait of a Lady,* and *Hercules and Antaeus*; and by Piero, *Temperance* and the *Portrait of Galeazzo Maria Sforza*.

Above, left: Cimabue's Santa Trinita Madonna, and, on the right, Giotto's Ognissanti Madonna. Facing page, above: the Battle of San Romano by Paolo Uccello; below: the diptych with the Dukes of Urbino by Piero della Francesca.

Room 10-14 (The Botticelli room). Some of the greatest masterpieces of the artist and of the entire 15th century are hung here, including the famous *Primavera* (1477-78), the *Birth of Venus* (1486) the realistic *Adoration of the Magi*, the touching *Annunciation* and the sophisticated *Madonna of the Magnificat* and the *Madonna of the Pomegranate*. Mention should also be made of the festive colorful *Adoration of the Magi* by Filippino Lippi and panel paintings by Lorenzo di Credi and Ghirlandaio.

Room 15 (Dedicated to artists active between the 15th and 16th centuries, known also as the Leonardo room). Among the works on exhibit let us recall Verrocchio's *Baptism of Christ*, Leonardo's *Adoration of the Magi* and his *Annunciation*.

Room 16 (Room of the Maps). Works exhibited here include important paintings by Hans Memling, such as the *Madonna and Child Enthroned with two Angels*, *Saint Benedict*, the stupendous *Portrait of a Man* and *Portrait of Benedetto Portinari*.

Room 17 (Room of the Hermaphrodite). This small room contains the sculpture of the *Hermaphrodite* and the group of *Cupid and Psyche*.

Room 18 (known also as the Tribune). Its name was determined by the magnificent *tribune* by Buontalenti (1585-89). In addition to examples of antique sculpture,

the room contains a vast collection of 16th-century portraits including Andrea del Sarto's enigmatic *Portrait of a Lady* and outstanding portraits by Bronzino, Pontormo, Rosso Fiorentino and many other Mannerist artists. The center of the room is dominated by the *Medici Venus*, a first century B.C. copy of a Greek original of the 5th century B.C.

Room 19 (The Signorelli and Perugino Room). Noteworthy is the *Holy Family* and the famous *Madonna and Child* by Signorelli, and some intense portraits by Perugino, including those of *Don Biagio Milanesi* and *Baldassarre Vallombrosano*, and that of *Francesco delle Opere*.

Room 20 (Dürer and German Painting). The room contains exemplary portraits by Lukas Cranach the Elder including the famous *Portrait of Luther* and of his wife *Caterina Bore*, that of *Friedrich III* and *Johann I, Elector of Saxony*. But the most important artist represented is Albrecht Dürer with his *Adoration of the Magi*, the *Apostle Philip*, the *Large Calvary* and the deeply moving *Portrait of his Father*.

Room 21 (The Bellini and Giorgione Room including Venetian 15th-century painting). Outstanding are

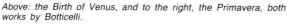
Above: the Birth of Venus, and to the right, the Primavera, both works by Botticelli.

Giovanni Bellini's imaginative *Sacred Allegory*, and Giorgione's two masterpieces, *Moses undergoes Trial by Fire* and the *Judgement of Solomon*.

Room 22 (Flemish and German Masters). To be noted are the *Adoration of the Magi* by Gerard David and the *Portrait of Sir Richard Southwell* by Hans Holbein.

Room 23 (The Correggio Room). Particularly striking are the *Madonna and Child in Glory*, the popular and tender *Rest on the Flight into Egypt*, and the moving *Adoration of the Child*, all by the founder of the Emilian school, Antonio Allegri called Correggio. Also

of interest are two portraits attributed to Raphael's early years, the portrait of *Elisabetta Gonzaga* and that of *Guidobaldo da Montefeltro*.

And finally Andrea Mantegna's *Triptych* with the *Epiphany*, the *Circumcision* and the *Ascension*, as well as his small and touching *Madonna delle Cave*.

Room 24 (The Room of Miniatures). This room contains a number of Italian, French, German and English miniatures dating from the 15th to the 18th centuries.

Room 25 (The Michelangelo Room). In addition to important paintings such as Mariotto Albertinelli's *Visitation*, his *Annunciation* and *Nativity*, and Rosso Fioren-

tino's *Moses Defends the Daughters of Jethro*, attention centers on the *Holy Family* or *Doni Tondo* by Michelangelo.

Room 26 (The Raphael and Andrea del Sarto Room). The room contains a wealth of masterpieces including Andrea del Sarto's *St James* and his statuesque *Madonna of the Harpies* and, above all, Raphael's *Pope Leo X with Cardinals Giulio de' Medici and Luigi de' Rossi*. Raphael's transparent *Madonna of the Goldfinch* is also particularly lovely.

Room 27 (The Pontormo and Rosso Fiorentino Room). Note particularly Pontormo's haunting *Supper at Em-*

maus and Rosso Fiorentino's intimate *Madonna and Child*.

Room 28 (The Titian Room) The room contains a wealth of masterpieces by the great Venetian painter: the penetrating *Portrait of Bishop Ludovico Beccadilli*, the famous *Venus and Cupid* and the *Portraits of Eleonora Gonzaga della Rovere* and *Francesco Maria della Rovere*. But the finest of all is the *Venus of Urbino*.

Room 29 (The Parmigianino Room). In addition to various important works by painters such as Luca Cambiaso, Girolamo da Carpi, Beccafumi and Perin del Vaga, the room contains various masterpieces by Parmigiani-

no such as the *Portrait of a Man, Madonna and Child with Saints* and the elegant sophisticated *Madonna of the Long Neck*.

Room 30 (Emilian Painting). This room houses works by Emilian artists of the 16th century, such as Niccolo Pisano, Niccolo dell'Abate, Dosso Dossi.

Room 31 (Room of Dosso). In addition to the *Sorcery* by Dossi, the room contains various works by Sebastiano del Piombo and Lorenzo Lotto.

Room 32 (Room of Sebastiano del Piombo). In addition to a fine *Sacra Conversazione* by Lorenzo Lotto and the *Portrait of a Knight* and the *Portrait of a Man* by Paris Bordone, note should be taken of Sebastiano del Piombo's famous *Death of Adonis*, influenced by Raphael in the softness of color and by Michelangelo in the powerful forms.

Room 33 (16th-century Painting and Foreign Artists). In particular mention should be made of the powerful portrait of *François I of France on Horseback* by François Clouet, *Christ Carrying the Cross* by Luis de Morales, a painting imbued with realism and human suffering, as well as a goodly number of paintings by Florentine artists of the late 16th century.

Room 34 (The Veronese Room). Particularly striking are the *Holy Family with Saint Barbara* (in restoration), with its warmth and intense vibrant colors, the small *Saint Agatha Crowned by Angels*, and above all the *Annunciation*, all by Veronese. Mention should also be made of Moroni's famous *Portrait of a Man with a Book* and the mystical *Transfiguration* by Savoldo.

Room 35 (The Tintoretto and Barocci Room). This room contains some of the masterpieces by late Mannerist painters: a penetrating *Portrait of a Man* by Tintoretto, his *Portrait of Jacopo Sansovino* and his soft *Leda and the Swan*. Together are to be found various paintings by Federico Barocci, represented by his large canvas of the *Madonna del Popolo*, his *Noli Me Tangere*, and then his *Portrait of a Girl* and the *Stigmata of St. Francis*.

Room 41 (The Rubens Room) Imposing canvases of

Above: *Annunciation* by Leonardo da Vinci; below: Raphael's *Madonna of the Goldfinch (del Cardellino)*. Facing page: Michelangelo's *Doni Tondo*.

Henry IV at the Battle of Ivry and the *Triumphal Entrance of Henry IV into Paris*, both by Rubens, are hung here. Mention should also be made of a fine series of *Portraits* by Van Dyck, Sustermans and Rubens.

Room 42 (The Niobe Room). The statues of the group of the *Niobids* discovered in Rome in 1583 and trans-

ferred to Florence in 1775 are on exhibition here. The statues are Roman copies of Hellenistic originals of the 3rd and 2nd centuries B.C.

Room 43 (The Caravaggio Room). Three basic works by Caravaggio at once strike the eye: the *Medusa*, the *Adolescent Bacchus*, and the dramatic *Sacrifice of Isaac*.

Room 44 (The Rembrandt Room). The room contains various masterpieces by Rembrandt: the two lovely *Self-Portraits*, as an old man and as a young man. Note also Rembrandt's famous *Portrait of an Old Man*, also called *The Rabbi*.

Room 45 (Painting of the 18th Century). This is the last room in the Gallery. A number of 18th-century works, particularly by Italian and French painters, are on ex-

hibit here. There are canvases by great *vedutisti* (panorama painters) such as Canaletto, Bellotto and Francesco Guardi, and expert artists from north of the Alps such as Jean Baptiste Simeon Chardin and Jean Etienne Liotard as well as a series of portraits by Rosalba Carriera. Between the door leading to Room 25 and the one leading to Room 34 is the entrance staircase to **Vasari's Corridor**, built by Vasari in 1565 and joining the Gallery to Palazzo Pitti. Along the Corridor are hung important paintings by Italian and non-Italian artists and the entire painting collection of *Self-Portraits* (Raphael, Titian, Bernini, Rubens, Rembrandt, Velazquez, Canova, David, Ingres, Corot, Delacroix, and many others) up to the artists of the 20th century.

Above: the Ponte Vecchio. Facing page, above: Palazzo Pitti, and, below, the Iliad Room inside the Palatine Gallery.

PONTE VECCHIO

The oldest bridge in the city, it was built as it is now in 1345 by Neri di Fioravante, with its elegant three-arched span. A characteristic feature of the bridge is the rows of small houses on either side. At about the center of the span over the river, the buildings are interrupted and an opening furnishes a fine view of the Arno and the other bridges. A bronze bust of *Benvenuto Cellini* has been placed here. Above the houses, on the upstream side of the bridge, is **Vasari's Corridor**, built by Vasari so Cosimo could go from Palazzo Pitti to Palazzo Vecchio.

PALAZZO PITTI

Palazzo Pitti is the most imposing of the city palaces and dates to 1457 on a probable design by Brunelleschi; in the 16th century the Medicis commissioned Ammannati to enlarge it. Access to the **interior** is through the great portal with its central arch which leads into a charming Doric atrium by Pasquale Poccianti (1850). This leads to Ammannati's famous **courtyard**, at the back of which is the **Grotto of Moses**, carved in porphyry by Raffaele Curradi; antique Roman statues are set under the arcades at the sides, while to the right is the **Chapel** frescoed by Ademollo with a magnificent *altar* of inlaid pietra dura work and a fine *Crucifix* by Giambologna. The *scalone d'onore*, lined with antique busts, begins on the same side of the courtyard; on the landing is the *Medici Genius* by Giambologna; the

first floor goes to the vestibule of the **Royal Quarters** and the **Galleria Palatina**. On the second floor is the **Galleria d'Arte Moderna**. The portico in the right wing of the facade of the palace leads to the **Bacchus Courtyard**, the current main entrance to the Galleria Palatina and the Museo degli Argenti, with the *fountain of Bacchus* by Cioli, which portrays the court dwarf of Cosimo I.

PALATINE GALLERY

The Palatine Gallery is the second museum in the city, both for size and interest, after the Uffizi, and it contains works of art that are enormously important for the history of art. It was constituted by Ferdinando II de' Medici who commissioned Pietro da Cortona to decorate various rooms of the Gallery. As time passed, the collection - a typically 17th-century picture gallery with the walls entirely covered with pictures in keeping with the taste of the times - was enlarged by Cardinal Leopoldo de' Medici and, later, by the last members of the Medici family and by the Lorraine Grand Dukes. The Gallery consists of a series of rooms dedicated to gods and mythological figures, represented in the decoration. The visit begins with the **Castagnoli Room** (decorated by Castagnoli, 1784) which contains Sodoma's *Saint Sebastian*, with the saint mystically meditating on his suffering. Turning right you will find yourself in the **Volterrano Apartments**, dedicated to the painter who frescoed the five *Allegories* on the walls. Next come the **Fine Arts Room**, the **Hercules Room**, the **Aurora**

Above, left: the Portrait of Agnolo Doni, and, to the right, the Madonna of the Chair, both works bt Raphael in the Palatine Gallery. Facing page, above: Boboli gardens, and, below, the Palazzina of the Forte di Belvedere.

Room, the **Berenice Room** and the **Room of Psyche**, which house works by Tuscan 17-century painters. Continuing straight ahead from the Castagnoli Room we enter the **Music Room** with frescoes by Luigi Ademollo; then to the **Poccetti Gallery** (frescoes by Poccetti) which contains paintings by Rubens and Spagnoletto among others, and then to the **Prometheus Room** (ceiling by Giuseppe Collignon, 1842) with an outstanding lifelike *Madonna* by Filippo Lippi. From here, keeping to the right, we come to the **Gallery of the Columns**, with many works by Flemish painters on the walls; then to the **Hall of Justice**, which contains the *Portrait of a Man* by Titian and various intense *Portraits* by Bronzino, and lastly to the **Room of Flora**. Back in the Prometheus Room we continue our itinerary with the **Ulysses Room**, which contains Raphael's famous *Madonna dell'Impannata*, Andrea del Sarto's *Madonna and Child with Saints* and other important paintings; on to the **Education of Jupiter Room** in which Caravaggio's famous *Sleeping Cupid* is to be found; the lovely **Iliad Room** (decoration by Luigi Sabatelli, 1819) where various authentic masterpieces are on exhibit, including one of Raphael's most famous pictures, the *Portrait of a Woman* known as *La Gravida* (1508), Andrea del Sarto's mystical *Assumption of the Virgin* (1519), the *Portrait of a Woman* by Ridolfo del Ghirlandaio, Titian's intense introspective *Portrait of a Man* and his *Philip II of Spain*, and the *Portrait of Philip IV of Spain* by Velazquez. The **Saturn Room** (ceiling by Ciro Ferri) contains works by Raphael, including the *Portraits of*

Angelo and maddalena Doni, the austere *Portrait of Cardinal Bernardo Dovizi da Bibbiena*, the acute *Portrait of Cardinal Inghirami*, the softly modelled *Madonna and Child*, known as the *Madonna del Granduca*, the *Madonna of the Baldachin* and the tender *Madonna of the Chair*; to be noted in particular in the **Jupiter Room** (ceiling by Pietro da Cortona, 1643-45) is the *Madonna del Sacco (Madonna of the Sack)* by Perugino, Andrea del Sarto's *St. John the Baptist*, the powerful and intense figure of *Saint Mark* by Fra Bartolomeo, the *Annunciation*, once more by Andrea del Sarto, the charming *Holy Family* by Rubens, and the enigmatic delicate *Portrait of a Woman*, known as *La Velata*, by Raphael. The **Mars Room** (ceiling by Pietro da Cortona, 1646) houses Murillo's *Madonna and Child* and *Madonna of the Rosary*, the famous *Consequences of War* by Rubens, the *Portrait of Daniele Barbaro*, a glowing painting by Veronese, Titian's *Portrait of Cardinal Ippolito de' Medici* and Van Dyck's *Cardinal Luigi Bentivoglio*; to be noted in particular in the **Apollo Room** (ceiling by Pietro da Cortona, 1660) is Titian's sensuous *Magdalen*, the dramatic *Deposition* by Andrea del Sarto, the *Portrait of Vincenzo Zeno* by Tintoretto and Rosso Fiorentino's *Madonna Enthroned with Saints*. Particularly striking in the **Venus Room** (ceiling by Pietro da Cortona, 1641-42) is the *Portrait of a Woman*, known as *La Bella*, by Titian, his *Portrait of Pietro Aretino*, one of the outstanding achievements of the Renaissance, and the lively painting of *Ulysses Returning from the Island of Phaecia* by Rubens.

BOBOLI GARDENS

The Boboli Gardens comprise the largest monumental green space in Florence. The history of the gardens goes back four centuries. In 1549 Cosimo I de' Medici commissioned them from Niccolò Pericoli, called Tribolo. After his death the undertaking was continued and added to by Ammannati, Buontalenti, and finally Alfonso Parigi the Younger. Today entrance to the gardens is through the **Bacchus Courtyard** beyond which is the evocative **Buontalenti Grotto** (1583), an artificial grotto consisting of various chambers covered with artificial incrustations and frescoes. Further up is a large basin called **Neptune's Pond**, with at the center a fine bronze statue of Neptune by Stoldo Lorenzi (1565). From here a steep alley, known as the *Viottolone*, leads to the **Piazzale dell'Isolotto** with the stupendous *Oceanus Fountain* by Alfonso Parigi (1618) at the center of a charming garden.

FORTE DI BELVEDERE

The Forte di Belvedere, or of St. George, was commissioned from Buontalenti (1590-95) by Ferdinando I. The building, set on a hilltop south of the Arno, dominates the city and the river from within its star-shaped fortifying wall. The protected access rises through an entrance hall to the terrace in front of the **Palazzetto** which is now used for exhibitions and art manifestations. An opening in the bastions communicates with the Boboli Gardens below.

31

CHURCH OF SANTO SPIRITO

The church of Santo Spirito founded in 1250 received its present form in the 15th century when it was built according to a model by Brunelleschi who had conceived it as a twin to the church of San Lorenzo. The **facade** however was never finished and is still only a rough plastered wall with an undefined silhouette at the top. The fine **dome** was designed by Brunelleschi, while the soaring **bell tower** is by Baccio d'Agnolo (1503). The **interior** is one of the finest examples of Renaissance architecture, a Latin cross with three spacious aisles.

CHURCH OF SAN LORENZO

Consecrated by St. Ambrose in 393, S. Lorenzo was the oldest church in the city. It was then rebuilt along Romanesque lines in 1060. The present building dates to 1423 and was designed and built by Brunelleschi. The

Left: the facade of the Church of Santo Spirito; below: the complex of the Church of San Lorenzo and the Medici Chapels.

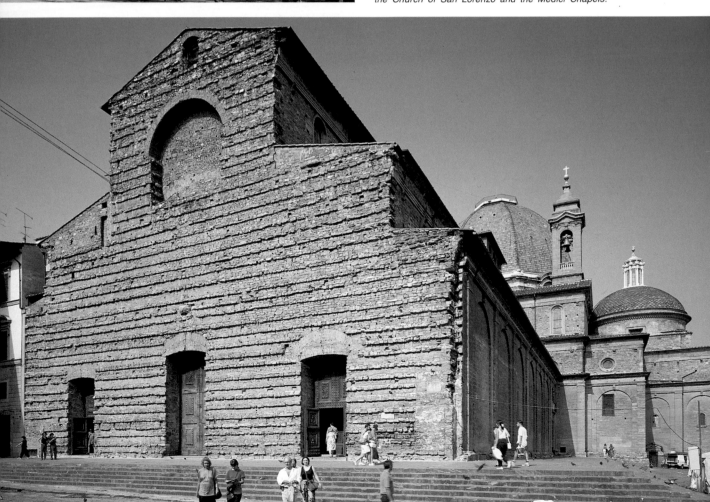

simple bare **facade** lacks the marble revetment: Michelangelo's design was never carried out. The **internal facade** which Michelangelo also designed is comprised of three doors between two pilasters with garlands of oak and laurel and a balcony on two Corinthian columns. The **interior** has a nave separated from the side aisles by Corinthian columns. The ceiling has magnificent gilded rosettes in white ground coffering. The **Sacrestia Vecchia** or Old Sacristy at the back of the left transept was built by Brunelleschi between 1419 and 1428. Earlier than the church, the sacristy is the first example of early Renaissance architecture and of the work of Brunelleschi in Florence. A dome covers the square room and a square apse opens off one wall. The structural lines are stressed by stone molding. Eight roundels by Donatello (1435-1443) with the *Four Evangelists* and *Scenes from the Life of St. John* are set into the pendentives and the lunettes.

SACRESTIA NUOVA

This room, designed by Michelangelo around 1520 and now connected to the **Medici Chapels**, overturns the restrained equilibrium of Brunelleschi's room, in San Lorenzo. Facing the tomb with the *altar* designed by Michelangelo is the *sarcophagus of Lorenzo the Magnificent and Giuliano de' Medici*, above which are the statues of *St. Damian* (by Raffaello di Montelupo), the *Madonna and Child* (by Michelangelo) and *St. Cosmas* (by Giovannangelo Montorsoli). The *tombs of Giuliano, duke of Nemours*, and *of Lorenzo, duke of Urbino*, face each other at the center of the other walls. Michelangelo placed the sarcophaguses with the reclining *Allegories of Time* under the statues of the dukes, set in niches: Giuliano's tomb is watched over by *Day* and *Night* while *Dusk* and *Dawn* watch over Lorenzo's.

Below; left: the Tomb of Giuliano, duke of Nemours, watched over by Day and Night; right: the Tomb of Lorenzo, duke of Urbino, with Dusk and Dawn. Both groups, by Michelangelo, are in the Sacrestia Nuova.

The facade of Santa Maria Novella, a 15th-century work by Leon Battista Alberti.

CHURCH OF SANTA MARIA NOVELLA

Begun in 1279 by Sisto da Firenze and Ristoro da Campi, it was finished in 1348 by Jacopo Talenti with the campanile in Gothic style (1330). The marvelous **facade** was finished between 1456 and 1470 by Leon Battista Alberti, who designed the portal and the part above it divided into compartments by inlaid marble and framed by the coats of arms (sails of fortune) of the Rucellai who commissioned the great work. The **interior** is subdivided into a nave and two aisles by piers carrying pointed vaults. In the second bay of the **right aisle** is the *tomb of the Beata Villana*, by Rossellino (1451), and the **Cappella della Pura**, a Renaissance structure built

in honor of a miracle-working *Madonna*, a 14th-century fresco, in the left-hand corner. In the right arm of the crossing is the terra-cotta *bust of St. Antoninus* and, above, the *tomb of Tedice Aliotti, Bishop of Fiesole*, by Tino di Camaino. Steps lead to the **Rucellai Chapel** with remains of frescoes of the *Martyrdom of St. Catherine* by Giuliano Bugiardini; at the center of the pavement is the fine *tomb-plate for Leonardo Dati* by Ghiberti (1423). From the crossing there is access to the **Bardi Chapel** and the **Chapel of Filippo Strozzi the Elder** with important frescoes, including scenes from the *Lives of St. Philip and St. John Evangelist* by Filippino Lippi (1503). On the back wall is the *tomb of Filippo Strozzi*

34

by Benedetto da Maiano (1491); the **Chancel (or Cappella Maggiore)**, with frescoes on the vault and on the walls with scenes from the *Lives of St. John the Baptist* (on the right) and *of the Virgin* (on the left) by Domenico Ghirlandaio (late 15th century). Then come the **Gondi Chapel**, decorated by Giuliano da Sangallo, the **Gaddi Chapel** and the **Chapel of the Strozzi family of Mantua**. Masaccio's *Trinity*, an extremely important fresco, is in the **left aisle**; on the second pier is a *pulpit* designed by Brunelleschi. The gate to the left of the facade leads to the Cloisters of the Large Convent: the **First Cloister**, the famous **Spanish Chapel** by Jacopo Talenti (1359), the **Chiostrino dei Morti** (Cloister of the Dead) and the **Chiostro Grande**.

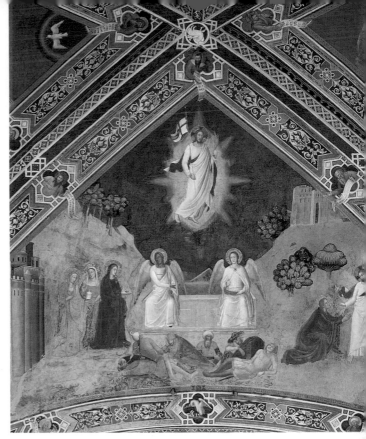

Adjoining: a view of the vault of the Spanish Chapel; below: part of the Spanish Chapel with the 14th-century fresco by Andrea di Buonaiuto depicting the Church Militant.

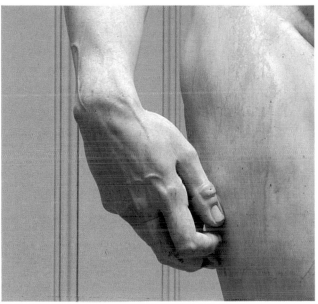

Facing page: Michelangelo's David inside the Tribune of the Accademia. This page, above: details of David's head and of his hand; right: one of Michelangelo's "Prisons".

GALLERIA DELL'ACCADEMIA

The Gallery houses an extremely important collection of sculpture by Michelangelo. The room that leads to the tribune, hung with tapestries, contains the *Palestrina Pietà*, whose attribution to Michelangelo is controversial, the unfinished *St. Matthew*, made for the Florentine cathedral, and the four «*Prisons*» (or slaves) which were meant for the tomb of Julius II in St. Peter's in Rome, which was never finished, like these male figures who seem to be trying to free themselves from the marble grip. At the center of the spacious *Tribune* is the original of the *David* (1501-4) commissioned from the great sculptor to replace Donatello's *Judith* on the balustrade of the Palazzo dei Priori. The room also contains an important collection of *paintings* of the Tuscan school of the 13th and 14th centuries. Three small rooms are to the right of the Tribune and contain various *shrines* attributed to Bernardo Daddi and a fine *Pietà* by Giovanni da Milano. To the left is another series of three small rooms containing works by famous masters of the 14th century. To the left of the Tribune another large *hall* contains works of the Florentine 15th century. Giambologna's *Rape of the Sabines* (1583), formerly in the Loggia dei Lanzi, is also now in the Gallery.

CHURCH AND CONVENT OF SAN MARCO

The Convent was mentioned as early as the 12th century. In 1437 Cosimo the Elder commissioned Michelozzo to re-build it and the convent of San Marco was therefore the first to acquire the elegant terse forms of the Renaissance. The fine **Cloister** is a simple stone structure with brick cornices. Light arcades delimit the space on the ground floor. On the first floor are fine *lunettes* frescoed by Poccetti, Rosselli, Coccapani, Vanni, Cerrini, Dandini, but most of the frescoes are by Fra Angelico who passed the greater part of his life within these walls. A staircase leads to the next floor with Fra Angelico's famous *Annunciation* at the head; off the corridor is the splendid **Library** by Michelozzo. The **Church** was restored in 1437 by Michelozzo himself; it was later remodeled by Giambologna (1580) and then by Silvani; the simple facade was redone between 1777 and 1780. The *interior* is austere and the carved and gilded ceiling is of note. On the door is a *Crucifix* of the school of Giotto, while there are many works on the altars. Nearby is Michelozzo's **Sacristy**, the **Chapel of St. Antoninus** and the **Cappella del Sacramento**.

Left: the Church of San Marco; below: the lunette with Fra Angelico's Crucifixion, inside the Convent of San Marco. Facing page, above: the Chimaera of Arezzo, an Etruscan bronze; below, right: the François Vase, an Attic krater from Chiusi.

ARCHAEOLOGICAL MUSEUM

One of the most important museums of its kind in Italy for the wealth of its collections which include examples of Egyptian, Etruscan, Greek and Roman antiquities. The **Egyptian Collection** was begun in 1824. Some of the most interesting items include the striking statue of the *goddess Hathor nursing the Pharaoh*, the polychrome relief of the *goddess Hathor with the Pharaoh, Sethos I*, the bas-relief of the *goddess of Truth Maat* and the *funerary statue of the priest Amenemhet*. The **Etruscan section** comprises an immense amount of material collected in over three centuries of study. There are a great number of sarcophagi, cinerary urns, bronzes, weapons and objects of daily use. Particularly striking in the field of sculpture are the famous *Chimaera*, the statue of the orator known as the *Arringatore*, and the statue of *Minerva*. The **Graeco-Roman section**, even though considerably smaller, includes very important pieces such as the bronze statue known as *Idolino*, a Greek work of the 5th century B.C. Of great interest is the vast **Collection of vases and terracottas** of Italic, Etruscan and Greek make (including the famous *François Vase*, a Greek work of the 6th century B.C. found in an Etruscan tomb), as well as the sections of **Eastern Mediterranean culture**, **Prehistory** and rooms with the *copies of the frescoes from the Etruscan tombs of Orvieto*.

The Bargello palace, surmounted by the tower known as "Volognana", and next to it the spire of the bell tower of the Church of Badia.

Facing page: above, the Room with pieces of 14-century sculpture; below, the upper loggia.

MUSEO DEL BARGELLO

The Bargello palace was built in 1255 as the headquarters of the Capitano del Popolo. The **interior** opens around the courtyard with porticoes on three sides. A picturesque **open staircase** leads to the upper **loggia**. Since 1859 the palace has been the seat of the **Museo Nazionale** which contains Renaissance sculpture and masterpieces of the minor arts from various periods. Mention is mandatory on the ground floor of the spacious **Entrance Hall**, the **Courtyard** and the **Room** which contains the interesting pieces of 14th-century sculpture. Important works by Michelangelo are housed in a hall nearby: the *Bacchus* (1496), the *Pitti Tondo*, the *David* or Apollo (1530), *Brutus* (1540). To be noted around these are works by Ammannati, Tribolo, Danti, Francavilla and Sansovino. In the same room there is also a bronze *Bust of Cosimo* by Cellini, and Giambologna's *Mercury*. The first room to the right at the top of the open staircase is now the **Donatello Room**, which contains many of his works including *St. George* (1416), the young *St. John*, the marble *David* (1408), and the bronze *David*. Also by Donatello is the *Marzocco* and the *Cupid-Attis* in bronze. In addition to works by Luca della Robbia, Ghiberti, Vecchietta and Agostino di Duccio, the room also contains the panels which Ghiberti and Brunelleschi made in 1402 in the competition for the second doors for the Baptistery in Florence.

CHURCH OF SANTA CROCE

The church is one of the city's largest and has a neo-Gothic **facade** added on in the 19th century with a heavy superabundance of ornamentation. The building, attributed to Arnolfo di Cambio, has a majestic tripartite **interior**. In the **right aisle** is the famous *Madonna del Latte*, a bas-relief by Antonio Rossellino. On the wall are the *funeral monuments of Michelangelo Buonarroti*, by Vasari (1564), *of Vittorio Alfieri*, poet and patriot, by Canova (1803), and *of Niccolò Machiavelli* by Innocenzo Spinazzi (1787). The church also contains the octagonal pulpit by Benedetto da Maiano (1477); a tabernacle in *pietra serena* with the *Annunciation* by Donatello (1472-76); the *tomb of the historian Leonardo Bruni*, by Rossellino; the *funeral monument to Gioachino Rossini* and the one to the poet *Ugo Foscolo* by Antonio Berti (1939). In the **Castellani Chapel** or «*Chapel of the Sacrament*», in the right arm of the transept, is the cycle of frescoes by Agnolo Gaddi (1385). Further on, at the head of the transept, is the **Baroncelli Chapel** with inside, on the right wall, the fine fresco of the *Madonna of the Girdle with St. Thomas*,

View of the complex of Santa Croce. On the facing page: the Cappella Maggiore inside the church with the polyptych of the Madonna and Saints by Niccolò Gerini.

by Bastiano Mainardi (1490) and the cycle of *Scenes from the Life of Mary*, by Taddeo Gaddi, on the other three walls; on the altar is the fine *Coronation of the Virgin* by Giotto. Michelozzo's portal in the right side of the transept leads to the **Sacristy**, originally built in the 14th century, and with *Scenes from the Passion* by Niccolò Gerini on the right wall. In the central or east wall of the Sacristy is the **Rinuccini Chapel** with scenes from the *Lives of the Virgin* and of *St. Mary Magdalen* by Giovanni da Milano and a fine *altarpiece* by Giovanni del Biondo (1379).

Various chapels with important works of art open off the back of the central part of the transept: the **Velluti Chapel** with *Scenes from the Legend of St. Michael Archangel*, perhaps by Cimabue; the **Bellacci Chapel** with a lunette-shaped vault with *Scenes from the Life of St. Andrew Apostle* by Giovanni da San Giovanni; the **Silvestri Chapel** with the *monument to Carlotta*

Above: the interior of the Church of Santa Croce; left: the Pulpit by Benedetto da Maiano. Facing page, above left: the Funeral Monument to Michelangelo, designed by Vasari; right: the Tomb of Galileo Galilei by Foggini; below: Giotto's fresco of the Funeral Rites for Saint Francis in the Bardi Chapel.

Buonaparte, by Lorenzo Bartolini; the **Peruzzi Chapel** with the magnificent *Scenes from the Life of St. John Evangelist* by Giotto (1320); the **Bardi Chapel** with the *Scenes from the Life of St. Francis* by Giotto (1318), then comes the **Cappella Maggiore** (Chancel) with the *Legend of the True Cross* (1380) by Agnolo Gaddi. On the altar is a polyptych with the *Madonna* and *Saints* by Niccolò Gerini and, above the altar, a *Crucifixion* or Triumphal Cross, of the school of Giotto; next comes the **Tosinghi Chapel** with, on the altar, a *polyptych* by Giovanni del Biondo; the **Benci Chapel**; the **Ricasoli Chapel**; the **Pulci Chapel**; the **Bardi di Vernio Chapel**. At the far end of the left arm of the crossing are the **Niccolini Chapel** and the **Salviati Chapel**. The *tomb* of the humanist *Carlo Marsuppini* by Desiderio da Settignano, and of *Galileo Galilei* (1642) by Foggini are in the left aisle. At the back of the **Cloister** is the marvelous **Pazzi Chapel** which Brunelleschi designed on a central plan with a dome and a lantern. The ribbed *dome* and lantern are set above the walls articulated by pilasters. Entrance to the former **Refectory** and the **Museo dell'Opera di Santa Croce** is from the First Cloister.

GALILAEVS GALILEIVS PATRIC. FLOR.
GEOMETRIAE ASTRONOMIAE PHILOSOPHIAE MAXIMVS RESTITVTOR
NVLLI AETATIS SVAE COMPARANDVS
HIC BENE QVIESCAT
VIX. A. LXXVIII. OBIIT. A. CIƆ. IƆ. C. XXXXI.
CVRANTIBVS AETERNVM PATRIAE DECVS
K. VIRE. PATRICIIS SACRAE IVIVS AEDIS PRAEFECTIS
MONIMENTVM A VINCENTIO VIVIANO MAGISTRI CINERI BONOQVE SIBIVI.
TESTAMENTO E.I.
VERE(I) IV BAPT. CLEMINS NELLIVS IO. BAPT. VENETTIVS E.
LVDENTI ANIMO ABSOLVIT.
AN. CIƆ. IƆ. C. C. XXXVII.

Above: a panorama of the Piazzale Michelangelo with the copies of works by Michelangelo. Facing page: the striking facade of the Church of San Miniato.

VIALE DEI COLLI AND PIAZZALE MICHELANGELO

The **Viale dei Colli** (Hill Avenue) winds for about six kilometers on the heights around the south side of the city, providing panoramic spots with fascinating views. It was laid out in 1868 by the architect Giuseppe Poggi who also made the plans for the **Piazzale Michelangelo**, an enormous terrace overlooking Florence. In the piazzale are copies of Michelangelo's sculptures: *David* and the four *allegorical figures* on the Medici tombs in the New Sacristy of San Lorenzo.

In the background, set above the piazzale, is the **Palazzina del Caffè** (1873), also by Poggi, which partly conceals the churches of S. Salvatore and S. Miniato al Monte.

CHURCH OF SAN MINIATO

The lower part of the **facade** is decorated with fine arches; the upper part is simpler and has a fine 12th-century mosaic with *Christ between the Madonna and St. Miniato*. The **inside** is tripartite with a trussed timber ceiling. On the walls are fragments of 13th and 14th-century frescoes. The large **crypt** closed by a *wrought-iron gate* of 1338 is outstanding. Returning from the crypt note should be taken of the raised **Presbytery**, which has a fine *pulpit* (1207) and inlaid wooden *choir stalls*. In the conch of the apse is a large mosaic of *Christ between Mary and St. Miniato* (1277). To the right of the presbytery is the entrance to the **Sacristy**, completely frescoed by Spinello Aretino (1387) with sixteen *Scenes from the Legend of St. Benedict*.

SCOPPIO DEL CARRO

Of particular significance to the people is an event which takes place during Easter mass in the Duomo: the Scoppio del Carro or Explosion of the Cart. A sort of wooden pyramid on wheels, the cart, is drawn by two oxen up to the front of the Duomo, while in the neighboring Church of the SS. Apostoli the ecclesiastic authorities light a large votive taper using the stones which the Florentine Pazzino de' Pazzi brought back from the first crusade, and which are said to come from the Holy Sepulcher. A spark is produced when they are rubbed together. The taper is carried in procession to the inside of the Duomo, and the Bishop, surrounded by the Town authorities and the trumpeteers in costume, uses it to light a rocket in the shape of a dove which "flies" towards the cart. When it arrives there is a noisy colorful explosion of firecrackers and Catherine wheels, with the appearance of flags and banners. According to tradition, the rapidity or slowness of the flight of the dove is an indication of the outcome of the harvests for that year.

CALCIO IN COSTUME

This football game in 16th-century costume is an ancient tradition that was brought back to life in the 1930s and which since then has become an annual event. This old ball game is played in the Piazza della Signoria with four teams participating in furiously disputed matches. Each team represents a different city quarter and wears a distinguishing color.

FIESOLE

This ancient city of Etruscan origins lies at the top of a hill overlooking Florence. The town centers around the lovely **Piazza Mino da Fiesole** with the large **Cathedral of S. Romolo** dating to the 11th century, which contains the important Cappella Salutati, frescoed in the 15th century by Cosimo Rosselli and the *Tomb of Bishop Salutati* by Mino da Fiesole. The **Palazzo Vescovile** (11th cent.) and the old **Church of Santa Maria Primerana** lie across from the Cathedral. From here one can go up towards the **Church** and the **Franciscan Convent** (14th cent.), which houses the **Ethnographic Mission Museum** which contains important Etruscan material. It is but a short walk from the piazza to the **Museo Civico Archeologico** and the lovely **Roman Theater** dating to the first century B.C. where important theatral and cinematographic manifestations are held. Nearby are the **Roman Baths** and the **Etrusco-Roman Temple**. Not to be forgotten is the valuable **Museo Bandini** which houses sculpture and painting from the 13th to the 15th centuries, and the very old **Basilica of San Alessandro.**

Facing page, above: the Explosion of the Cart in front of the Duomo; below: a moment in a football match (calcio in costume).

Right: the small church of San Francesco in Fiesole and, below, the Roman theater in Fiesole.

PRATO

One of the most important industrial cities in Tuscany, Prato has an interesting historical center. The spacious **Piazza del Duomo** is surrounded by old buildings. At the center stands the marvelous **Cathedral of S. Stefano** in Romanesque style, dating to the 12th century. Outside the Cathedral is the splendid *Pulpit of the Holy Girdle*, a work by Donatello set on a bronze capital by Michelozzo. The *Pulpit* in the nave is also of great interest. It was made by Mino da Fiesole and Rossellino (1473) together.

Near the Cathedral is the **Palazzo Vescovile** which houses the **Museo dell'Opera del Duomo** with important works by Donatello and Paolo Uccello. In the **Piazza del Comune** are the fine **Palazzo Comunale** and the **Palazzo Pretorio**. The latter houses the **Galleria Comunale** with its fine collection of paintings, including works by Filippo Lippi, Filippino Lippi, Luca Signorelli and Giovanni da Milano. Of note among the other churches is the **Church of San Francesco** (13th cent.) which contains the *Monument to Inghirami* by Rossellino, the **Church of Santa Maria delle Carceri**, by Giuliano da Sangallo (1484-95) and the **Church of San Domenico** (13th cent.). The **Castle of the Emperor**, which dates to the 13th century and was built for the Emperor Frederick II of Swabia, is an imposing structure.

MEDICI VILLAS

Various splendid villas are to be found in the surroundings of Florence. They are living evidence of the power the Medicis attained. Sober and imposing, the buildings have their own individual personalities. Particular mention must be made of the **Medici Villa of Poggio a Caiano**, built for Lorenzo the Magnificent by Giuliano da Sangallo. The two building blocks are joined by a hall, a fine portico with piers which runs around the building, and a graceful staircase. The interior contains a wealth of 16th-century frescoes. **Villa Demidoff**, already late 16th-century in layout, looks quite different today. A few masterpieces are still to be found in the enormous park (open to the public), such as the *Colossus of the Apennines*, a gigantic statue executed by Giambologna between 1579 and 1580. **Villa La Petraia** was a medieval castle before being transformed into a Medici residence by Bernardo Buontalenti. Important frescoes by Volterrano are inside. The lovely garden contains a *Fountain* by Tribolo and a bronze *sculpture* by Giambologna. The **Medici Villa of Careggi**, which already belonged to the Medicis as early as 1417, was enlarged by Michelozzo in 1457. The **Medici Villa of Castello**, seat of the Accademia della Crusca, is built along powerful 15th-century lines. There are frescoes by Pontormo and Volterrano inside.

Facing page: above: the Emperor's Castle, and, below, the Cathedral of Prato. Above: the Villa of Artimino, and, below, the Medici Villa of Poggio a Caiano.

Above: a view of the town of Vinci; left: the Castle.

VINCI

The town is famous above all because it is the birthplace of Leonardo, the great genius who still today is why people come to Vinci. A fine **Museum** has recently been installed which serves as a study center on Leonardo's work as well and which houses numerous models of machines and contraptions made from designs by Leonardo. But the town is much older than its illustrious representative: it developed around the castle of the feudatory Counts Guidi and then in the 13th century passed under the dominion of Florence. Still today the **Castle** retains its 13th-century appearance: inside it is decorated with coats of arms and other ornaments. Within the walls of the castle is the **Church of Santa Croce**, Romanesque in origin but frequently remodeled. Also of interest is the 17th century **Oratory of the Santissima Annunziata**, on the site of a particularly venerated shrine. Inside is an *Annunciation* attributed to Paolino da Pistoia.

PISTOIA

Pistoia is situated on the northernmost extremity of the fertile plain of the Ombrone river, surrounded by the Arno, Monte Albano and the Apennine slopes. The city's charming small historical center contains extremely fine examples of architecture. The first inhabitants of the area were probably Etruscan but not until Roman times did Pistoia begin to take on the characteristics of a real town and even became a Roman *municipium*. The historical center is enclosed within the Medici walls built by Cosimo I. The heart of the city is the beautiful **Piazza del Duomo** with the **Cathedral** which dates to the 12th-13th century. The lovely facade has a spacious porch with an important bas-relief in glazed terra cotta by Andrea della Robbia in the vault. The tripartite interior contains various artistically noteworthy works by artists such as Verrocchio and Lorenzo di Credi. Next to the Cathedral is the **Museo del Tesoro** with interesting examples of goldwork and religious furnishings.

Right across from the Cathedral is the **Baptistery**, a small octagonal building in black and white marble built to a project by Andrea Pisano in the first half of the 14th century. This lovely building in Gothic style has three finely decorated portals and a gallery of polylobate blind arcading at the top of the wall just below the dome. The lintel of the main portal is sculptured in low relief with *Stories of St. John the Baptist* and the lu-

The 13th-century Palazzo Comunale of Pistoia, seat of the Museo Civico.

nette above contains a *Madonna and Child* with at the sides two fine statues of *St. John the Baptist* and *St. Peter* by the school of Andrea Pisano.

Next to the Cathedral is the **Palazzo Comunale**, dating to the late 13th century, with a Gothic-arch porch on its severe facade. The **Museo Civico** inside contains important works of art from the 13th to the 15th centuries. Right across from the Palazzo Comunale is the **Palazzo Pretorio** or of the Podestà, dating to the 14th century, with a simple decisive architecture. Lastly, next to the Cathedral, is the **Palazzo dei Vescovi** (11th cent.) with a lovely facade in Gothic style, and eight pointed-arch openings on the first floor while the second floor has elegant two-light openings.

Other outstanding historical buildings include the **Church of San Giovanni Fuorcivitas** of which only the left side still retains elements of the original Romanesque structure while the facade is part of a 14th-century enlargement. Inside, the Church contains a fine *Visitation* attributed to Andrea della Robbia, a *polyptych* by Taddeo Gaddi and a *holy water font* by Giovanni Pisano. The Renaissance **Church of the Madonna dell'Umiltà** is also truly lovely. The building consists of two rooms: the atrium and an octagonal structure. Mention must also be made of the **Church of San Francesco**, an imposing building in Gothic style with a Latin-cross interior and frescoes by Lorenzetti, Puccio Capanna and Lippo Memmi. The **Church of Sant'Andrea** (12th cent.) has a fine portal with a statue of *St. Andrew* in the manner of Giovanni Pisano in the lunette. The tripartite interior contains Giovanni's famous *pulpit*. Also meriting attention are the **Ospedale del Ceppo** (13th-14th cent.), the **Church of Santa Maria delle Grazie** (15th cent.), the **Abbey of San Bartolomeo in Pantano** (12th cent.), the **Palazzo dei Capitani del Popolo** (late 13th cent.), and the **Medici Fortress**, a Renaissance structure.

Left, above: the Cathedral of Pistoia, and, below, a detail of the arch over the portal. The delicate glazed vault by Andrea della Robbia has a Madonna and Child, by the same artist, at the back. Facing page, above: the Baptistery of Pistoia and the Palazzo Pretorio; below: the loggia of the Ospedale del Ceppo with reliefs from the Della Robbia workshop.

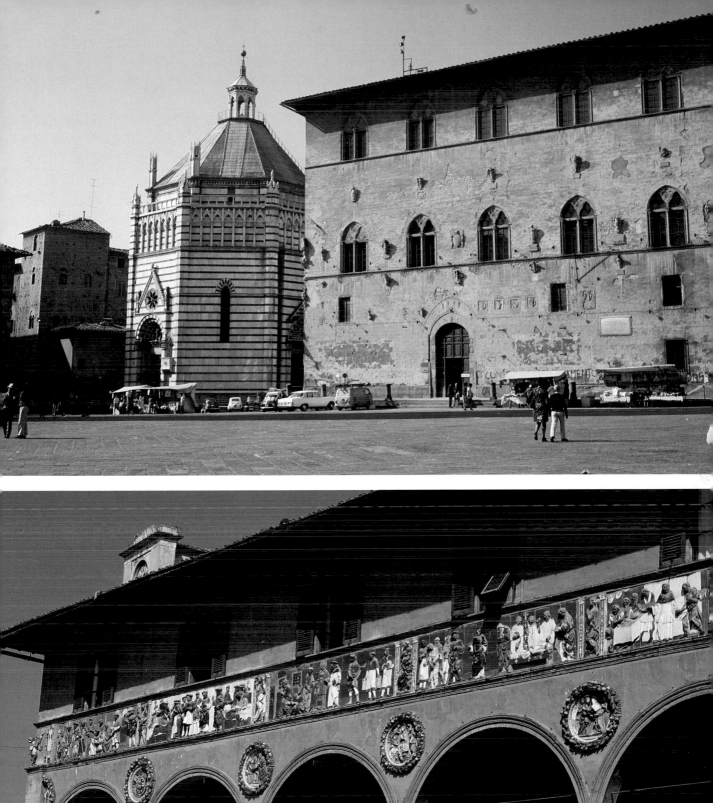

Above and left: shots of the ski runs near the Abetone.

ABETONE

One of the most famous winter resorts in the Tuscan Apennines is Abetone, which lies 1388 meters above sea level and is provide with hotels and facilities for the great number of mountain enthusiasts who come year round. Crowned by an immense forest of firs, larches, Scotch firs, beeches, maples and birches, it includes various localities: **Boscolungo, Consuma, Le Regine, Chirofonte** and **Serrabassa**. Numerous excursions and climbs can be made from Abetone. The many fine ski runs are often used for high level competitions.

MONTECATINI TERME

The city lies in a vast plain at the far end of the Val di Nièvole. It is famous for its *spas* and has eight springs of prevalently sulphate-alkaline water, an authentic cure-all for disorders of the liver and the digestive apparatus. Particularly charming is the center of **Montecatini Alto**, an old castle-town situated on a hill behind Montecatini Terme.

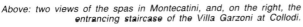
Above: two views of the spas in Montecatini, and, on the right, the entrancing staircase of the Villa Garzoni at Collodi.

COLLODI

Splendid estates lie in the pleasant surroundings of Pistoia as they do around any important city. These include **Villa Forti** in Chiari and **Villa Cecchi**, known as the Guardatoia, but the finest of all is the imposing **Villa Garzoni** (now Gardi dell'Ardenghesca), built between 1633 and 1662 on the site of a medieval castle in a typically Luccan Baroque style. Behind the villa lies the town of Collodi whose fame is in part due to the fact that the Florentine writer Carlo Lorenzini (1826-90), the author of *Pinocchio*, used the name as his pseudonym. He passed his childhood here in the town his mother was born in. In its labyrinth of lanes, Collodi retains a medieval character, clustered around the **Church** that was founded in the 14th century and the ruins of the **keep**. Not far from Villa Garzoni, near the **Osteria del Gambero Rosso**, designed by Giovanni Michelucci in 1963, is the **Park of Pinocchio** with the *monument to Pinocchio and the Fairy* by Emilio Greco (1956), the **Piazzetta dei Mosaici** by Venturino Venturini and the **Paese dei Balocchi** (Land of Toys) where Pinocchio's adventures are enacted.

LUCCA

Lucca was founded on a flood plain that stretches from the last foothills of the Tusco-Emilian Apennines to the northern uplands of Monte Pisano, not far from the river Serchio. This ancient noble city has a wealth of picturesque towers and churches of the time of the communes, Renaissance palaces, fascinating streets. The oldest part of the city is enclosed in the circuit of walls which are still in good condition and which give the city its typical aspect. In Roman times it was an important *municipium*; the city then was taken by the Goths and subsequently by the Lombards and the Carolingians. In 1119 the city managed to become a free commune and its period of prosperity began. The **Cathedral** stands in the Piazza San Martino. It was built in the 12th century in Romanesque style, but was completely remodelled in the 14th and 15th centuries. Three large arches of different size, resting on composite columns, are in the lower part of the facade, which is still Romanesque, while above these there are three tiers of loggias. The tripartite interior has important works of art such as the famous *Tomb of Ilaria del Carretto* and the statue of *St. John the Evangelist*, both by Jacopo della Quercia, as well as works by Tintoretto, Civitali, Ghirlandaio. The **Treasure of the Opera del Duomo**, composed of a

Below: the Guinigi tower in Lucca, with a holm oak on the top; right: an aerial view of the Piazza dell'Anfiteatro.

great number of religious objects in gold and silver dating to the 14th-15th centuries, is situated inside the complex.

Not far off is the **Baptistery**, a small 14th-century building with a square ground plan and a Gothic dome; the **Church of San Giovanni** (12th cent.), considerably modified in the 17th century; the *Monument to Maria Louisa of Bourbon* (1834); the **Palazzo della Provincia**, an unfinished work by Ammannati. **Palazzo Mansi** (17th cent.) rises up in the Via Galli Tassi. It contains many magnificent richly-furnished rooms, including the lovely *Camera degli Sposi*, an 18th-century alcove with carving in Baroque style. The palace houses the **Pinacoteca Nazionale** with works by artists ranging from the Renaissance to the 19th century, such as Luca Giordano, Bronzino, Salvatore Rosa, Veronese, Tintoretto and many others. Nearby stands the Renaissance **Church of San Paolino**, with important 15th- and 16th-century works. Not far off is the imposing silhouette of the **Palazzo Pretorio**, begun in 1492 by Civitali, and the lovely **Church of San Michele in Foro** (12th-14th cent.), an example of pure Pisan-Luccan Romanesque architecture. The splendid facade has four tiers of loggias and the tripartite interior has a perfectly round apse.

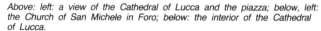

Above: left: a view of the Cathedral of Lucca and the piazza; below, left: the Church of San Michele in Foro; below: the interior of the Cathedral of Lucca.

The church contains notable works of art by Andrea della Robbia and Raffaello da Montelupo. Another striking religious building is the **Church of San Frediano** (12th-14th cent.) with a fine tripartite facade enhanced by a mosaic of the *Ascension*. The **Piazza dell'Anfiteatro** lies right across from the church. It is characterized by the fact that it stands on the site of a Roman amphitheater of the second century A.D. The **Church of San Pietro Somaldi** (13th cent.) has a fine facade in Pisan Romanesque style and a unique bell tower in brick. Turning into the Via Guini, two rows of brick buildings, known as **Case Guinigi**, are worthy of note. Shortly thereafter comes the **Church of Santa Maria Forisportam** (13th cent.), a fine example of Pisan Romanesque with an essentially linear facade in marble with arcading and loggias.

Mention must also be made of the **Palazzo Bernardini**, and the lovely **Villa Guinigi**, which houses the **Museo Nazionale** divided into two main sections: archaeology (Etruscan, Roman and Ligurian material) and painting (including sculpture, paintings and the minor arts). Lastly, the most fascinating feature of the city are its **Walls**, built between the 16th and 18th centuries. They continue for about five kilometers and are still completely viable.

In the two photos, various stretches of the bulwarks and the city walls of Lucca.

BARGA

The city was the heart of the Medici Grand Duchy in Garfagnana. The religious buildings of the city are particularly interesting: first and foremost the **Cathedral**, built and modified in various stages from the 9th to the 20th century. No less interesting are the 16th-century **Church of San Francesco**; the numerous **palaces** which belonged to the important local families and which line the Via di Mezzo, di Borgo and Pretorio; and the **Palazzo Pretorio**, seat of the Florentine podestà who set their *coats of arms* on the 14th-century loggia next to the building.

BAGNI DI LUCCA

The municipality of Bagni di Lucca is composed of various townships along the Lima and the hills. In the Middle Ages the waters of Bagni di Lucca were already known, but the **Spa Establishments** began to go up in the 15th century. In the 19th century the spa was frequented by Louis of Bourbon, thus attracting the Tuscan nobility and various personalities such as Byron and Shelley.

BORGO A MOZZANO

A small agricultural and industrial town, Borgo a Mozzano still retains interesting signs of its past including the **Parrocchiale of San Jacopo**, which contains some

Left: the pulpit in the Cathedral of Barga; below: view of Bagni di Lucca. Facing page: the Devil's Bridge at Borgo a Mozzano.

Above: the shores of the Lake of Massaciuccoli near Torre del Lago; left: the house of the maestro, Giacomo Puccini. Facing page, above: the beach of Viareggio, and, below, the walkway with the Teatro Margherita.

15th-16th century sculpture and some interesting Della Robbian terra cottas; the **Oratory of the Crucifix**, with a fine wooden *Crucifix* of the 16th century, and the **Church of San Francesco** in Baroque style. Not far from the town is the picturesque **Bridge of the Devil** or **Ponte della Maddalena**, with a hog's back roadbed and asymmetrical arches (14th cent.).

TORRE DEL LAGO

The small town became famous in the early 1900s due to the presence here of the Luccan composer **Giacomo Puccini**, who built his residence on the shores of the lake. Today his **villa** lies only a few meters from the water and contains musical and hunting mementos of the master in the dusky rooms, furnished in the Art Nouveau style then in fashion. The bust in the small square overlooking the lake is also dedicated to Puccini. Every summer in Torre del Lago there is an interesting musical event, the *Puccini festival*, during which there are open air performances of the great composer's most famous operas.

VIAREGGIO

Some of the loveliest buildings still to be seen in Viareggio that date to the early 1900s are the **Bagno Balena** and the **Teatro Margherita**, while 19th-century Viareg-

gio is represented by the majestic **Palazzo delle Muse**, which overlooks Piazza Mazzini and now houses the **Museo Civico Archeologico A.C. Blanc**. Very little is left of the old 16th-century town, except for the imposing **Torre Matilde**, built after 1534 as a result of an ordinance by the Luccan senate. The first masonry structures of the small port were built around this defense tower. As time passed the port continued to grow in importance thanks both to commercial fishing and to shipbuilding, activities which still today play an important part in the local economy, side by side with the flourishing resort activities. Lastly, speaking of Viareggio mention of its famous *Carnival* is mandatory. The imaginative floats take the masters in the art of papier machè months to make.

FORTE DEI MARMI

Today Forte dei Marmi is the most elegant tourist resort on the entire Versiglia coast and is, without doubt, one of the most famous vacation spots in Italy. This town, known in antiquity solely as the point of arrival for precious marbles from the Apuans, is now famous for the development of its tourist facilities in the 1900s. But one sign of its obscure past still remains, the **Fort**, built by Grand Duke Pietro Leopoldo around the end of the 18th century to defend the zone from barbarian incursions.

Left: the Torre Matilde in Viareggio; below: a moment in the famous Carnival of Viareggio. Facing page: two images of Forte dei Marmi with, above, the building of the Fort in the city center.

MASSA

Situated on one of the low hills which block the narrow valley of the stream Frigido, at the foot of the Apuan Alps, Massa is about five kilometers from the sea. The city contains various interesting examples of medieval and Renaissance architecture. Important buildings in Massa include the **Palazzo Cybo Malaspina**, which was begun in 1557 on what remained of a precedent Malaspina villa; the **Cathedral**, originally 13th-century, but heavily remodelled and restored in the course of time; and the **Museo Storico di Arte Sacra**, annexed to the Cathedral. Note should also be taken of the 18th-century **Church of the Carmine** and the **Malaspina Castle**, which consists of a large complex including the **Rocca Malaspiniana** which dominates the entire city, as well as the fortress, built between the 15th and the 16th century.

Above: the Palazzo Cybo-Malaspina in Massa; left: the facade of the Cathedral. Facing page, above: the Malaspina Castle looming over the city with, below, a stretch of the beach of Marina di Massa.

CARRARA

The town is separated from Massa by the hills of Candia. The torrent Carrione runs through the town which is situated below the Apuan Alps. Carrara is the city of marble; its inexhaustible quarries have been known for over 2000 years. The city is proud of its **Marble Museum** which exhibits samples of the various types of marble to be found in the Apuan Alps, and of the **Palazzo Cybo Malaspina** with its 16th-century layout, the seat of the **Accademia delle Belle Arti**. Next to the **fountain of Andrea Doria** or of the Giant, a lovely unfinished work by Baccio Bandinelli, is the **Cathedral**, begun in the 11th century and completed two centuries later. It is completely covered with a facing of grey and white marble and is partly Romanesque and partly Gothic. The 13th century **campanile** is a fine example of Ligurian architecture. The tripartite interior of the church is ornamented with 12th- and 13th-century *frescoes* and important sculpture.

Left, above: a view of the port of Marina di Carrara; below: Piazza Alberiga in the city center of Carrara. Facing page: two views of the Apuan Alps, dotted with marble quarries (below).

PISA

Pisa lies 13 kilometers from the sea on a vast flood plain protected on the northeast by Monte Pisano where the lower Valdarno joins the coastal plain. The origins of Pisa are still now uncertain. Some Latin historians, including Livy, claim that it was founded by the Ligurians. Others, including Servius, maintain that it was built by Phocaean merchants. Whatever the case may be, Pisa does not seem to have fully developed until Roman times when we know it was an ally of rome in the Second Punic war, a Roman city in 89 B.C. and a flourishing colony in the times of Augustus.

In 641 it fell under Lombard dominion and was strategically important in that it was the first and only port the Lombards controlled until they succeeded in taking possession of Genoa.

Under the Carolingian dynasty it became part of the *marchesato* of Tuscany but, even though a subject city, it was actually autonomous enough to suceed in becoming a free Commune at the beginning of the 11th century. This was the beginning of an extremely prosperous period in its history which lasted almost three centuries. The city became a powerful center thanks to the control of the seas by its relentless fleet. In this period Pisa became an ally of the Normans and aided them in their conquest of Sicily. It participated in the first crusade with 12 ships and founded numerous merchant colonies in the East, expanding its commercial dominion. In the 12th century the city was at the acme of its fortunes. Pisa won a great victory over the Muslim fleet and later defeated its rival Amalfi. Evidence of this felicitous period are the many religious and profane buildings which sprang up in the city. Work on the Cathedral was begun and urban growth led to a restructuring of the city walls. Artistically, too, Pisa became a great cultural center, above all thanks to the genius and personality of sculptors such as Nicola Pisano, his son Giovanni Pisano, and Arnolfo di Cambio, all of whom, together with a goodly group of other illustrious artists, created schools which were held to such account that they served as example throughout Italy.

A slow but inexorable decline began with the 13th and 14th centuries, caused by the continuous clashes on land with its neighbors Lucca and Florence and on sea with its bitter rivals Genoa and Venice. In the 15th century Florence, ever more powerful, set its eyes on Pisa and after various struggles and vicissitudes Pisa became subject to the Medici city. In addition, the building of the port of Livorno (Leghorn), which in the meantime was becoming another rich marine power, deprived Pisa of her supremacy over the seas and definitely sanctioned the city's decline. But Pisa was not a city to be overcome. Defeated on a military and political level, it reconfirmed its status as a great city of culture, one of the most important university centers. In fact it was no

Adjacent: an aerial view of the Piazza dei Miracoli in Pisa, with the Baptistery and the Cathedral flanked by the Camposanto Monumentale, and, in the background, the Leaning Tower.

less a figure than Galileo Galilei who initiated a prestigious scientific tradition which then continued under the Lorraine dynasty. In 1860 Pisa became part of the Kingdom of Italy. Today, small and self-contained as it is, concentrated around its center, it is a city rich in cultural ferments, stimulated by a flourishing economy that depends above all on the activity of the pharmaceutical, textile and glass industries and by an unceasing tourism.

CATHEDRAL

The construction of the Cathedral of Pisa to all extents and purposes took place in the second half of the 11th century. The **interior plan** consists of a nave and four aisles, like the largest early Christian basilicas in Rome, but with a projecting three-aisled transept. Women's galleries run along over the side aisles and an octagonal dome is set at the intersection of the nave and transept.

A large apse terminates the nave and also each arm of the transept. Tall columns articulate the nave, interrupted by four piers which support the drum on which the dome rests, while the women's galleries above look out on the nave through broad two-light openings. The interior of this large church is luminous, enlivened by the vivacious polychrome decoration as well as by the play of darks and lights which derive from the complex spatial organization. The classic decoration of the capitals in Buscheto's construction are offset by the decidedly more Romanesque decoration with figures on the capitals that belong to the 12th- century prolongation of the Cathedral.

The outstanding work of art that enriches the primatial church of Pisa is the *pulpit* made by Giovanni Pisano in the first decade of the 14th century to replace the one by Gugliemo which was sent to Cagliari. The pulpit is hexagonal, on a circular base, and is carved with *Stories from the Lives of St. John the Baptist and Christ* in the

Above: the interior of the nave with the famous Pulpit by Giovanni Pisano (right).

Facing page: the elaborate facade of the Cathedral of Pisa.

panels which are divided by figures of *Prophets* and *Saints*. It is one of the finest expressions of Italian Gothic sculpture. There is also a lovely ivory statue of the *Madonna* by Giovanni in the **Treasury of the Duomo**. The Cathedral also contains the *tomb of Arrigo VII* by Tino di Camaino. It is however on the **exterior** that the splendor of multicolored marbles reaches its zenith. With the exception of the facade, the side walls and the clerestory form an uninterrupted succession of three tiers which encircle the monument. The **facade** also preserves testimony of the principal creators of the Duomo. In the first arch is the *sarcophagus-tomb of Buscheto*; above the central portal on the right, an *inscription* recalls Rainaldo, who began the facade; in the left pilaster, on the level of the sidewalk, is the *sepulchral inscription of Master Guglielmo*, the sculptor famous for the first pulpit of the Cathedral - a model that was long in use - and who with his workshop finished the upper part of the facade.

On this page: various details of the famous Leaning Tower. Facing page: an overall view which clearly shows how much it leans off center.

THE LEANING TOWER

The campanile of Pisa was begun in 1174 by Bonanno. At first the tower must simply have sunk down into the ground, but later it began to lean, perhaps as a result of attempts to remove infiltrations of water in the foundations. Therefore in 1185 when the tower had arrived halfway up the third story the work was interrupted. Building began anew in 1275 under the direction of Giovanni di Simone and in only nine years another three and a half floors were raised. Around the middle of the 14th century Tommaso Pisano was charged with terminating the tower with the present belfry after having leveled off the floor corresponding to the seventh cornice. In the late 1950s the movement of the tower had once more slowed up and the difference between the base and the top was then five meters and seventeen centimeters. At present the overhang increases by about a millimeter per year. All these vicissitudes in the construction of the tower did not alter Bonanno's original design, except for the height and the belfry. It is said that inspiration for the circular form of the tower came from Ravenna but it might also have come from the orient. The decoration is in any case related to the facade of the Cathedral, as is confirmed by the ground floor gallery of blind arches on engaged columns and the floors above with small galleries articulated by cornices.

BAPTISTERY

The building was begun in 1152 by Diotisalvi. The ancient chronicler Maragone informs us that in 1164 the columns were set up in only 15 days. In 1260, under the direction of Nicola Pisano, the gallery of small columns was added and the design for the Gothic facing is also his. It must be noted that around the middle of the century the main furnishings for the Baptistery were also in place: the baptismal font by Guido da Como in 1246 and Nicola Pisano's pulpit in 1260. After the middle of the 14th century the conclusive phase in the construction of the Baptistery went into effect when it was decided to cover the building with a dome.

Although the Baptistery, like the other monuments in Pisa, is based on a two-color scheme, the most important decorative feature is its sculpture. Examples are the decoration of the portals, especially the main portal which was given a *Madonna* by Giovanni Pisano in the lunette, and the rich decoration of the galleries where the *human heads* (now replaced by copies) at the imposts of the arches were in goodly part by Nicola and Giovanni Pisano. The imposing ground plan of the Baptistery of Pisa is circular and the **interior** consists of an annular nave covered with vaulting which rests on columns and piers. Over the nave there is a women's gallery which faces onto the interior through arcading supported by piers.

Left: the exterior of the Baptistery with its elegant marble decoration; below: the interior with the baptismal font and the Pulpit by Nicola Pisano.

Above: the side of the Camposanto Monumentale which faces onto the Piazza dei Miracoli; right: Madonna and Child, by Giovanni Pisano.

THE CAMPOSANTO MONUMENTALE

The Camposanto was begun in 1278 on a design by Giovanni di Simone who, in 1263, had also built the Hospital on the other side of the square. Entirely faced with marble in two delicate tonalities, the Camposanto is articulated on a rectangular gallery - the long south side marks the edge of the Piazza - around the field of the old cemetery. **Outside**, the gallery is closed by blind arcading springing from pilaster strips, with sculptured heads at the imposts of the arches. **Inside**, the gallery faces onto the field through an arcaded portico on piers and with slender four-light openings. The interior walls of the Camposanto were frescoed, especially in the 14th century, and other tombs were added to those of the illustrious Pisans. At the beginning of the 18th century antique sarcophagi, many of which had been used as tombs around the Duomo, were also transferred here. In the 19th century ancient and medieval material found in the city was also brought here so today the Camposanto is one of the most important museums in Pisa, thanks also to the important fresco cycles it contains.

Facing page, above: the Palazzo dell'Orologio; below: the Palazzo dei Cavalieri; above: the Church of Santa Maria della Spina set against a retaining wall on the Lungarno.

The north arm of the gallery contains the famous *Scenes of the Old Testament* by Gozzoli, the *Stories of St. Efisio* by Taddeo Gaddi and Spinello Aretino, and further frescoes by Antonio Veneziano and Andrea Bonaiuti. There are also various important sarcophagi of the 2nd-4th centuries A.D.

The west arm houses sculpture of the school of Giovanni Pisano such as the *monument to L. Ammannati* (1359) and the *Sepulcher of the Gherardesca* (1315). Also of importance are various Roman sarcophagi. Most of the works of art are in the north arm, including the fine frescoes by Piero di Puccio (1390). Of particular note is the famous *Hall of the Frescoes* with the magnificent *Triumph of Death*, *Last Judgement* and other frescoes by Buonamico Buffalmacco.

OTHER MONUMENTS IN THE CITY

Piazza dei Cavalieri is the "secular" heart of Pisa. To be noted in particular: the **Palazzo dei Cavalieri** (now seat of the Scuola Normale of Pisa) built in the 16th century by Vasari; the beautiful statue of *Cosimo I de' Medici* which stands in front of the palace; the **Palazzo dell'Orologio**, also by Vasari; the **Church of Santo Stefano dei Cavalieri** (1569); and the important fountain right across from the Palazzo dei Cavalieri, created by Pietro Francavilla in 1596. Of considerable importance is the **Museo Nazionale di San Matteo** with its collection of paintings and sculpture of Pisan school, including works by Masaccio, Donatello, Gentile da Fabriano, Simone Martini, Fra Angelico, Spinello Aretino, Gozzoli and Ghirlandaio; and the Museo dell'Opera del Duomo.

Among the numerous churches scattered through the city particular attention should be paid to the **Church of San Francesco** (13th cent.) which contains lovely frescoes by Taddeo Gaddi, Taddeo di Bartolo, and Pietro Gerini; the **Church of Santa Caterina** (13th cent.) with its marvelous facade in two-colored marble and with important works by Nino Pisano inside; the **Church of San Michele in Borgo** (14th cent.); the **Church of San Pietro in Vincoli** (1072-1119) and its magnificent four-aisled crypt; the **Church of San Martino** (14th cent.) with its fine marble facade and the splendid high relief of *St. Martin and the Poor Man* by Andrea Pisano; the **Church of the Holy Sepulcher**; the delicate Gothic **Church of Santa Maria della Spina**; the **Church of San Nicola** (13th cent.) which contains fine wooden sculptures by Nino and Giovanni Pisano; and the **Church of San Michele degli Scalzi** of Romanesque origin (11th cent.).

Above, left: the Basilica of San Piero a Grado; above: the Certosa of Pisa; left: the Cathedral of San Miniato.

SAN PIERO A GRADO

This majestic basilica in Romanesque style was built between the 10th and 13th centuries on the foundations of a precedent early Christian building. Legend relates that it was here, perhaps driven by a storm, that Saint Peter landed on his way from the Holy Land to Rome. The spacious building is one of the first examples of Pisan Romanesque architecture. The *frescoes* which line the walls of the nave are attributed to the Luccan painter Deodato Orlandi who worked in the basilica at the beginning of the 14th century.

CERTOSA DI PISA

Founded in 1366, this imposing complex of buildings includes the **Church**, the **Guest House**, the **Cloister**. The entrance vestibule leads into a large square dominated by the **Monastery** with the fine marble facade of the church at the center and the two flights of the long staircase.

SAN MINIATO

The town lies along the tops of three hills and most of it stretches out on either side of a single street. The majestic **tower of** ''**Frederick**'' rises up above the houses, while further down the **Cathedral** dominates the town. The **Museo Diocesano** has been opened next to the church and it contains many works from other

A stretch of the city walls of Volterra with the unique Porta all'Arco, an Etruscan work of the 3rd century D.C.

churches, churches in the diocese. But the religious building which best preserves its original features may be the **Dominican Church** dedicated to **Saints James and Lucy** (Santi Jacopo e Lucia), which dates to 1330. Also of interest is the **Palazzo Vescovile**, which overlooks the same square as the Cathedral and which was once the residence of the Capitano delle Milizie and has been the bishop's seat since 1622.

VOLTERRA

The earliest references to the city date to Villanovan times, that is to the iron age (9th-7th cent. B.C.). As *Velathri*, it was for a long time one of the most powerful lucumonies in Etruria. It was so important that in the 3rd century B.C. it had around 25,000 inhabitants and was the last lucumony to fall to the Romans after a siege that lasted two years (81-80 B.C.). The city was quite powerful between the 12th and 14th centuries when it often found itself fighting Pisa, Florence, Siena and San Gimignano for a question of territory and finally fell to the Florentines in 1361. One of Volterra's most pic-

turesque monumental areas is the Piazza dei Priori, framed by an austere mosaic of palaces: the **Palazzo del Monte Pio**, a solid elegant building that has recently been restored; **Palazzo Pretorio**, a union of several buildings dating to the 13th century; the **Torre del Podestà**, in the upper part of which a humorous beckoning figure of an animal, baptized by the inhabitants of Volterra the "porcellino" or piglet, stands on a ledge; the **Palazzo Incontri**, seat of the Cassa di Risparmio of Volterra (Savings Bank), in great part rebuilt in period style, and finally the **Palazzo Vescovile** with a unique overhanging roof.

Added to these is the **Palazzo del Popolo** or dei Priori, the first example of its kind erected in Tuscany. The facade, with many two-light windows and dotted with the polychrome coats of arms of the podestà, is crowned by the pentagonal tower. Open to the public, inside on the first floor is the **Sala del Consiglio**, decorated with a large late 14th-century fresco of the *Annunciation and Saints*, and the **Sala della Giunta** which has a beautiful wooden *ceiling*. The palace contains the civic offices and the **Picture Gallery** (Pinacoteca) with works by

Above: a view of the Rocca of Volterra. Facing page: panorama of Volterra with the Palazzo dei Priori in the foreground.

Volterran, Florentine and Sienese artists of the 14th to 17th centuries. The so-called **Porta all'Arco** is set into the Etruscan city walls on the south side of the city of Volterra, towards the sea. The front and back of the gate each have a large arch over four meters wide built in dry masonry with blocks of tufo. On the side facing away from the city three heads in dark stone, so weather-worn as to be illeggible, have been set into the arch. The **Cathedral** dates to the 12th century even though minor 13th-century changes are also evident. The **facade** is simple, linear, enriched by a finely decorated marble portal and blind arcading in the tympanum. The lovely **interior** consists of a nave and two aisles with columns and an exquisite coffered ceiling of the 16th century. The **Baptistery** is a 13th-century Romanesque building of great architectural interest that stands right across from the Cathedral. It is octagonal in shape. The portal, richly decorated with sculptured heads, leads into an interior that is striking in its spirituality. The large **Rocca-Fortezza** rises up at the end of the historical center. The structure consists of two parts that were once separate: the *Old Fort* (*Rocca Antica* or *femmina*) which dates to 1343 and which rises at one side of the Selci gate, and the *New Fort* (*Rocca Nuova* or *maschio*) which Lorenzo the Magnificent had built later (between 1472 and 1474). What remains of the imposing **Roman Theater** dating to the 1st century B.C. lies on the

north side of the city. A good part of the *scenae cavea* and the really fine portico are fairly well preserved. The **Baths**, which have mostly disappeared, were near the portico. Among the various museums and collections in the city note should be taken of the **Pinacoteca Comunale**, in the **Palazzo Solaini**, a building with a fine Renaissance facade and charming courtyard. Works by many renowned artists are on exhibit, including Luca Signorelli, Taddeo di Bartolo, Neri di Bicci, Ghirlandaio, Volterrano and many others. Works of great interest, most from Volterra and its diocese, are on exhibit in the **Museo Diocesano d'Arte Sacra**. Under the portico, at the entrance to the museum, is a collection of objects from the ancient abbey of the Camaldolesi. Among the most outstanding works in the museum: a *Madonna and Child with Angels*, a marble sculpture by Tino da Camaino; a *bust of St. Lino* in glazed terra cotta by Giovanni della Robbia; the *Conception*, a splendid panel painting by Taddeo di Bartolo. One of the main attractions in Volterra however is the **Museo Etrusco Guarnacci**. The museum includes a *Prehistoric section*, which contains material from the bronze age and iron age tombs; an *Etruscan section*, the most important both in quantity and quality (over 600 cinerary urns are included), and lastly the *Roman section*, with sculpture, inscriptions, objects in gold and pottery. One of the most important pieces on exhibition is the tufa *stele*

representing a warrior with a lance, of the second half of the 6th century B.C. Figures of demons, gorgons and geni, furies, Scylla and tritons, as well as representations of the journey to the underworld on horseback, are represented on the many cinerary urns. The most haunting piece is the famous «Shade of Evening», a long slender enigmatic figurine in bronze which dates to the second century B.C.

As usual, the **Etruscan necropolises** lie outside the city walls. Excavation is still being carried out in some of them. They include the *necropolis of the Portone*, with chamber tombs of the 6th-5th century B.C.; the *Guerruccia*, which has disappeared in the landslides of the Balze; the *Guardiola*; the *Marmini* with its two hypogeum tombs; and *San Girolamo*.

There have been frequent landslides in the area known as **Le Balze** to the west of the city, and these are responsible for its present appearance - an enormous chasm that falls away to the plain below. One by one these continuous landslides have swallowed up various stretches of the Etruscan walls (a magnificent panorama can be had from what survives) and many old buildings.

Left: a room in the Museo Guarnacci dedicated to the Etruscan cinerary urns; below: the chasm of the Balze. Facing page: a detail of the Statue of the Four Moors in Livorno.

LIVORNO

The origins of Livorno are uncertain: probably the zone where the city lies was already inhabited in neolithic times, as evidenced by various finds, but the real birth of the city is relatively recent. After Pisa fell to the Florentines (1405), Livorno passed under Genova which a few years later ceded it to Florence for 100,000 florins. This was the beginning of the city's prosperity. The population quadrupled and it rapidly became a very important port and the large Porto Mediceo was built - a fine structure which added luster to the city.

The city's **Cathedral** was built at the end of the 16th century on a project by Alessandro Pieroni, and was later enlarged in the 18th century. The simple **facade** is entirely faced with marble. The Latin-cross interior has a nave only and contains various fine *monumental tombs* such as the one dedicated to the Marchese Marco Alessandro del Borro and Count Ginori. The **Church of the Conception** is by Pieroni (1599). The facade is simple and restrained. The single-nave interior contains fine works of art including a bronze *Crucifix*, perhaps by Ferdinando Tacca, on the first altar to the right. The **Museo Civico Giovanni Fattori** is situated in a small palace at the center of the park of Villa Fabbricotti. It was founded at the end of the 19th century when it was decided to install the numerous collections donated to the city by Enrico Chiellini in a museum (prehistoric

Etruscan, and Roman archaeological material) and, later, various works by Giovanni Fattori and numerous other Macchiaioli artists were added. The coin collection is also of interest. The **Fortezza Vecchia** was built by Antonio da Sangallo the Younger between 1521 and 1534. In the interior is the small **Church of San Francesco** and archaeological material from the old Roman *castrum*. The **Statue of the Four Moors** is situated in Piazza Giuseppe Micheli and was dedicated to the Grand Duke Ferdinando de' Medici in 1596. The Four Moors, masterpieces by Pietro Tacca, an outstanding sculptor who worked at length for the prestigious Medici family, were not added until 1626.

The large **Medici Port** begins at the Piazza Micheli, continues along the street known as the Via del Molo Mediceo, where the old **Fortino della Sassaia** is situated, and reaches up to the wharf known as the **Molo di Cosimo**. On the other side of the wharf is an enormous basin with a large dam called the **Curvilinea**. Further north is the **Marzocco Dam**. Lastly, between the wharf and the curvilinear dam, which is built on rocks, the lovely 14th-century **Lighthouse Tower** rises towards the sky.

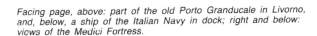
Facing page, above: part of the old Porto Granducale in Livorno, and, below, a ship of the Italian Navy in dock; right and below: views of the Medici Fortress.

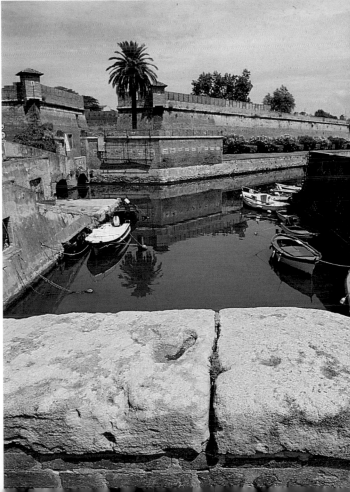

ACCADEMIA NAVALE OF LIVORNO

Founded in 1881 by Benedetto Brin, general of the navy, the Naval Academy combined the precedent academies of Genoa and Naples. Headquarters are in the palace built in 1878 on the remains of the old Lazzaretto di San Jacopo. The scope of the Academy is that of preparing the young officers who attend it for the Navy. Inside the building is the large monument presented by Austria in 1866 in memory of the famous naval battle of Lissa.

To one side and below: two views of the Amerigo Vespucci, training ship of the Naval Academy of Livorno.

Above: the complex of the Sanctuary of Montenero, right, one of the miraculous effigies of the Madonna with numerous ex-votos left by pilgrims.

MONTENERO

What has made Montenero unique as far as the Catholic church is concerned is the worship that countless numbers have dedicated to the mysterious and miraculous image of the Madonna brought to the uplands by a lame shepherd who was healed when he found it.

The Baroque richness of the **Church** centered around the miraculous effigy of the *Madonna and Child* has its counterpart in the adjacent rooms lined with an incredible number of *ex-votos* - an indescribable variety of relics which prove how strong faith is when accompanied by the sense of the supernatural.

Above: a view of Portoferraio. Facing page, above: part of the coast at Fetovaia; below: the small lake of Terra Nera, which is green because of the sulphur waters.

ISOLA D'ELBA

The largest island in the Tuscan Archipelago lies about ten kilometers from the continent. The coasts with their gulfs and bays are particularly beautiful. The highest of the many highlands on the island is Monte Capanne (1018 m.).

The island's economy is based on agriculture, tourism (which has greatly increased in the last years), fishing and the mining industries. The flavorful wines - red, white, muscatel and aleatico (sweet wines) - are much sought after.

Elba was already known by the Greeks who had discovered the immense deposits of iron. Later it was occupied by the Etruscans and then the Romans who left outstanding signs of their presence in the form of splendid villas and inhabited centers which still exist, such as Pomonte and Capoliveri (*Caput Liberum*).

After various vicissitudes in which the island passed first to the Medicis, then was contended between Spain and France, Elba was occupied by the English and three years later fell to the French. From 1814 to 1815 it was independent and Napoleon passed his exile here. It was then annexed to the Grand Duchy of Tuscany and in 1860 to the Kingdom of Italy.

Portoferraio is the chief town of the island; it has a small intimate historical center enclosed in a powerful 16th-century fortification. It is the principal port in Elba and also a famous tourist resort. Of the fine historical buildings in the center, mention should be made of the 16th-century **Parish church** and the **Town Hall**, which houses the **Biblioteca Comunale Foresiana**. Note also the **Church of the SS. Sacramento** with the *Madonna of the Assumption* by Giovanni Camillo Sagrestani on the ceiling; the **Church of the Misericordia** and the **Forte della Stella**. Other towns and villages on the island include **Capoliveri, Porto Azzurro, Rio Marina, Cavo, Marciana** and **Marciana Marina, Poggio** and **Marina di Campo**.

THE MAREMMA

This area extends from southern Tuscany as far as north-western Latium and is divided into **Maremma pisana** (north of Piombino) and **Maremma grossetana** (further south). In the interior it stretches out up to the western slopes of the Colline Metallifere for a total area of around 5000 square kilometers. The coastline is marked by the promontory of Punta Ala, Piombino and the Argentario. In ancient times it was the home of numerous powerful Etruscan cities. But with the fall of the Roman Empire, the Maremma went into an inexorable decline and the population diminished: the fields were abandoned and these forgotten lands for centuries became the realm of illness and malaria. Not until the extensive reclamation works promoted in 1828 by the grand duke of Tuscany Leopoldo II and the continuous and definitive salvage operations, organized in the early 1900s, did the Marem-

ma, by now almost totally reclaimed, once more become a fairly fertile land which can now lay claim to a discreet agricultural production, particularly in the field of animal husbandry.
Many well-known seaside resorts lie along the coasts, including San Vincenzo, Follonica, Marina di Grosseto, Punta Ala, Castglion della Pescaia, Porto Santo Stefano.

On this and the facing page: two stretches of the coastline of the Maremma; in the next two pages: herds of Maremman horses rounded up by the butteri.

95

Above and adjacent: phases in the "merca", the branding of the cattle by the butteri.

THE BUTTERO

The «*buttero*» is a characteristic figure of the Tuscan Maremma, who has always stimulated popular imagination. This almost mythical figure can be compared to the American cowboy: he is really none other than the Tuscan cowboy. His work consists in herding cattle along difficult winding routes, branding steers, breaking in the famous Maremman horses (an ancient race). Nowadays, what with progress, even the figure of the *buttero* has lost some of his legendary aura. Originally one of his most difficult tasks was the «*merca*» or branding which required great skill. The cattle had to be herded into a circular corral, in the middle of which was a forked pole, known as *giudice* (judge). The calf was lassoed and immobilized by several cowboys who held it fast by the tail, the horns and the hoofs. At this point the red hot iron branded the mark of the owner on the animal's flank. Now things are much simpler, but not nearly as fascinating, and the calf is immobilized by means of a system of corrals. The *buttero* as horse-breaker must also be gifted with intuition and skill. Breaking in an ordinary horse may not be easy, but breaking in a Maremman horse is a real challenge.

GROSSETO

Grosseto lies in the heart of the Maremma, near the right banks of the Ombrone river which winds its way through the vast plain. It is about ten kilometers from the sea. This prevalently modern city has spread out around the small compact historical center marked by the old Medici bastions.

As witnessed by an inscription, the **Cathedral** was begun in 1294 and finished early in the 14th century by Sozzo di Pace Rustichini, known also as Sozzo di Rustichino. The Cathedral was probably built on the remains of a Romanesque church, to judge from the pilasters with engaged columns set against the interior facade and the pilaster strips outside on the side walls. The facade, renewed in the 19th century, has three portals and an elegant loggia with a rose window above. The right side has a fine low-relief portal with a splendid sculpture by Cesare Maccari (1800), and, above, two two-light Gothic windows.

The interior has a nave divided from the two aisles by solid compound piers. At the end of still another bay is the apse, semi-circular outside but square inside. Of particular note in the second bay on the left is a fine

baptismal font by Antonio Ghini (1470-71) and, in the left arm of the transept, a lovely *altarpiece*, also by Ghini, with a splendid *Assumption* (15th cent.) by Matteo di Giovanni.

The **Museo Archeologico e d'Arte della Maremma** has a rich collection of archaeology and art. The Prehistoric section is installed on the ground floor with material from the paleolithic to the Villanovan periods. The Etruscan section presents material from the excavations of ancient settlements including Talamone, Vetulonia, Cosa, Sovana, Castro, Vulci, Pitigliano, Saturnia, Magliano and above all Roselle, where excavations are still under way in the ancient urban area. The upper floor contains the Topographical section where the material is arranged according to the river basin it comes from (Ombrone, Fiora, etc.). There is also a rich Collection of religious art on the second floor. Paintings of the Sienese school dating from the 13th to the 17th

Above: the Palazzo della Provincia in Grosseto. Facing page: the Cathedral of Grosseto.

Above: the interior of the Cathedral of Grosseto. Facing page, above: a stretch of the Medici Walls, and, below, a showcase with Etruscan pottery in the Museo Civico of Grosseto.

century include in particular a magnificent *Last Judgement* by Guido da Siena or his circle; a charming *Madonna and Child* by Segna di Bonaventura; a goodly number of works that can be ascribed to the circle of one of the above masters; a moving *Crucifixion* (first half of the 13th cent.) which is of such high quality that the name of Simone Martini comes to mind; the famous *Madonna of the Cherries* by Sassetta; and the two *Saints*, once wings of a polyptych, by Sano di Pietro. The collection also contains works by many other illustrious masters such as Girolamo di Benvenuto, Pietro di Domenico, Riccio, Vanni and Rutilio Manetti as well as a fine **Collection of ceramics**.

The austere 13th-century **Church of San Francesco** is in Gothic style. The gabled brick facade is enlivened by a portal with lunette and a fine rose window. The convent buildings were on the left side. Still extant is a Cloister with the so-called *well of the "bufala"*, built by Ferdinando I towards the end of the 16th century. Another well lies outside the church opposite the hospital. San Francesco has a single large nave with a trussed

timber roof and a fine terminal chapel. It contains a valuable *cross* set behind the high altar, perhaps an early work by Duccio da Buoninsegna (1289) and a lovely wooden *crucifix* (15th cent.) of Sienese school. The interior is partially lined with frescoes.

The **Medici Walls** were built in the second half of the 16th century and comprise a powerful bastioned circle of walls. At the beginning of the 19th century the glacis began to be transformed into public gardens and at one corner rises the **Medici Fortress** which incorporates the old **Sienese Keep** (a solid structure consisting of two distinct but interconnected parts with strongly escarped bases bordered by a string course). A fine view of the old town can be had from the fortress.

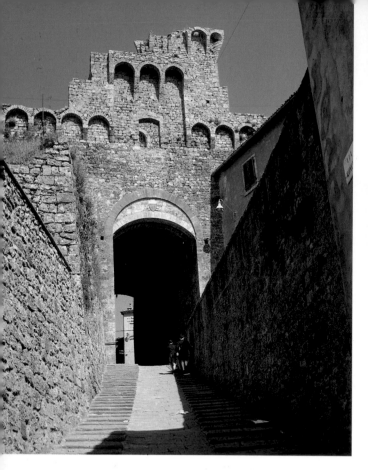

Above, left: the old portal of the Sienese Fort in Massa Marittima; right: panorama of the town with the Cathedral at the center. Facing page, below: the Town Hall.

MASSA MARITTIMA

This lovely town clinging to the hill that overlooks the open plain has many interesting witnesses to its past in the historical center. The town is now divided into the "old city" up on top and the "new city" further down, consisting mainly of modern buildings. Massa Marittima is probably of Etruscan origin but it became really important in the 9th century when it was chosen as a bishop's seat. In the Middle Ages it was one of the most flourishing free communes, thanks to the exploitation of the copper and silver mines nearby.

The city **Cathedral** is a lovely building in Romanesque style. Dating to the first half of the 13th century, it was then enlarged in the area around the presbytery and the apse between 1287 and 1304. The splendid facade has seven blind arches decorated with rhombs in the lower part. Travertine columns with Corinthian or composite capitals decorated with leaves or figures of animals divide the interior into a nave and two aisles. It contains various truly outstanding works of art.

The Romanesque-Gothic **Church of Sant'Agostino** dates to the early 14th century. The bare facade is in travertine and has a solid doorway with a finely decorated rose window above. Next to the facade is the **Cloister** and the embattled square campanile which dates to 1627. The interior with a nave only contains outstanding works of art by Lorenzo Lippi, Rutilio Manetti, and Empoli. The Romanesque-Gothic **Church of San Francesco** was built in the 13th century but the only part of the original structure left today is the polygonal apse. Once the residence of the Podestà, today the **Palazzo Pretorio** houses public offices. This solid austere building in travertine dates to the first half of the 13th century. The two upper floors are articulated by a row of two-light windows which enliven and illuminate the structure. The **Palazzo Comunale**, an imposing Romanesque building in travertine, has a fine series of two-light windows arranged in three floors. The building, which dates to the 13th-14th century, is actually the result of the fusion of several medieval tower-houses. Among the other monuments of interest mention must be made of the imposing **Sienese Fortress** built around 1335; the **Palazzo Vescovile**, completely rebuilt in 1814; the lovely **House of the counts of Biserno**, a fine Romanesque structure; the **Palazzo dell'Abbondanza**, which dates to the late 13th century; the **Archaeological Museum** with its interesting material from Etruscan tombs; and the **Museum of Minerology**.

Above: a stretch of the beach of Follonica. Facing page, above: the residential zone of Punta Ala; below: the town of Castiglion della Pescaia.

FOLLONICA

This industrial town is also a famous seaside resort, with an extensive beach bordered by a flourishing pine grove. The **Parish Church of San Leopoldo**, a church which dates to 1836-38, is interesting because of the original combination of materials used in its construction - cast iron, stone and wood. The **Biblioteca Comunale** is also of interest for its exhibition models of 19th-century smelting installations.

PUNTA ALA

This rocky zone lies at the southern tip of the gulf of Follonica. This patch of land is almost untouched, with a beach of fine sand crowned by a dense Mediterranean shrub which reaches down to the sea. In the last twenty years Punta Ala has become an exclusive residential area.

CASTIGLION DELLA PESCAIA

Well known seaside resort on the Maremman coast, Castiglion della Pescaia has a lovely beach and varied cliffs along the sea. The picturesque port-canal is always full of fishing boats and yachts. There is also a fine pine grove set above the city which here and there reaches right down to the sea. Clinging to a hillside and enclosed within a solid circuit of walls, the old medieval town of **Castiglione Castello** is dominated by the fine **Aragonese fortress** of the 14th-15th century.

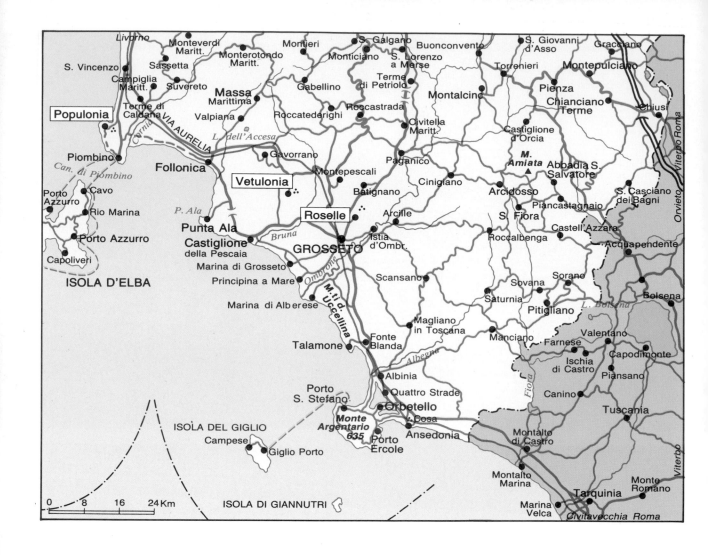

THE ETRUSCANS IN THE MAREMMA

The Maremma is one of the zones that the Etruscans originally occupied and some of their most flourishing cities rose here. A stable occupation of the area dates to the early iron age and can be explained by the presence here of both forests and minerals, and by the conformation of the zone both on the coasts and in the interior.

The small clusters of hut villages gradually developed until they became small cities which exploited the potentialities of the local resources which played an important part in the flow of trade which crossed Etruria in the 7th century B.C. But it was as sea-faring cities that they really flourished, for at the time the coast of the Maremma had many more inlets than it does now. In addition to the large Baratti Gulf, which is still a magnificent protected sheet of water, there used to be a vast internal marine lagoon, the so-called Prile Lake, on which both

Roselle and Vetulonia faced, and which then became a swamp. It has now been reclaimed and is part of the Plain of Grosseto.

Maritime links with the Island of Elba and the other coastal cities of Etruscan Latium are witnessed by finds of trade objects. From these it can be deduced that these cities flourished as long as the Etruscans maintained their supremacy over the seas, in other words until 474 B.C., when the Syracusan fleet defeated the Etruscans in the waters of Cumae. Some of the cities made a comeback between the 4th and 3rd centuries B.C., a period in which the Roman presence began to make headway, although without resistance. The founding in

Right, above: the entrance to the Tumulus of the Pietrera in Vetulonia. Below: part of the Etruscan necropolis of Populonia on the Baratti Gulf.

273 B.C. of Cosa, a Roman colony to be used as port of call, led in fact to the further decline of some of the ports and heralded the gradual Romanization of the area.

VETULONIA

Remains of the imposing Etruscan **circuit of walls**, constructed with enormous blocks of stone, can be seen in the medieval part of the town. The excavations of the urban center of Hellenistic-Roman times are right outside modern Vetulonia, at the **Costa Murata** and along the road that leads to the Aurelia. These paved streets, houses and shops, built in line with a well defined town plan with a sewage system, pavements, tubs and wells, date to the Etruscan-Roman period. But only the extensive necropolises can furnish an exact idea of the wealth and power of this center, from the 8th century B.C. on, when the copper, silver, and lead mines in the Colline Metallifere began to be exploited. The tombs of the ar-

chaic period, situated in the heights surrounding the city (**Poggio alla Guardia, Colle Baroncio, Poggio alle Birbe**, etc.) have rendered many objects in decorated bronze and locally made gold and silver jewellery, as well as precious handmade objects imported from the eastern Mediterranean area, Phoenicia, Egypt, Sardinia. Some of the richest tombs, both in the quality and quantity of the objects contained, include the **Circolo dei Monili, of Bes, of the Pellicce, of the Lebeti, of the Trident**, and the **Tomb of the Littore** and the **Tomb of the Duce**, dating to the late 8th- mid-7th century B.C. In the second half of the 6th century B.C. the monumental tumulus tombs of the nobility make their appearance, with square chambers and false vaulting supported by a central pier: two superb examples along the **Via dei Sepolcri** are the Tomb of the Pietrera and the Tomb of the Diavolina. The **Tumulus of the Pietrera** measures over 60 meters in diameter and has a long entrance corridor to the central chamber where various limestone statues of weeping women and male

Below: the bronze fan from the Tomb of the Flabelli in Populonia. Facing page: the Tomba Ildebranda at Sovana.

Above: bronze dolly with censer from Vetulonia; left: cinerary urn inside the Tomb of the Pellegrina in Chiusi. Facing page, above: golden fibula from Vetulonia; below: ivory comb from Marsiliana.

figures were found. On the slopes of the tumulus several pit tombs (*a fossa*) were brought to light. The precious objects they contained dated them to the same period (mid-7th century B.C.) as the main sepulcher. Not far off is the **Tumulus of the Diavolino**, of the same period, which takes its name from an animalesque figure incised on a stone next to the left jamb of the doorway. This sepulcher too, with its large tumulus delimited by the drum in blocks of stone, has a false vault which was supported in the center by the pier of which only the base is still extant. The following centuries have not left many traces, but a few recent finds seem to indicate that life in Vetulonia continued uninterruptedly throughout the 6th and 5th centuries B.C., to blossom out into a new period of prosperity in the 3rd century B.C.

POPULONIA

The ancient *Pupluna* was the only Etruscan city situated on the sea. The port, located in the **Gulf of Baratti** below the promontory on which the city stood, was already a center for exchange and trade in Villanovan times. Subsequently, with the exploitation of the iron mines on the island of Elba, the economy of the city reached considerable heights. The oldest necropolises of Populonia are located on the opposite sides of the gulf, at **Poggio delle Granate** and at S. Cerbone, and might indicate the earlier presence of two distinct villages

Above: open tombs in the tufa bed in the countryside of Sovana. Facing page, above: the Tagliata Etrusca near Cosa; below: the coast near Talamone.

which were later fused into the original nucleus of the Etruscan city. The tombs of the period (9th-8th cent. B.C.) are the classical "well" tombs (*a pozzetto*); as time passed the tombs became architecturally more evolved and with richer and more abundant tomb furnishings. In the Orientalizing period (7th cent. B.C.) there was a radical change in the types of funeral structures which tended towards monumentality, as witnessed by the chamber tombs of the **Costone della Fredda** and of the **Porcareccia**, but above all by the imposing tumuli of **S. Cerbone**. Among the most important of the funeral monuments mention must be made of the **Tomb of the Chariots** (dei Carri), the most imposing in the necropolis of S. Cerbone. This tomb, marked by a large cylindrical drum constructed in blocks of stone, and with stone slabs to carry off the rain water, is topped by a large tumulus of earth. It contained the remains of two war chariots with bronze and iron fittings, goldwork, objects in ivory, and bronze and iron arms which date the burial to around the middle of the 7th century B.C. Other tombs in the necropolis of S. Cerbone include the **Tomb of the Cylindrical Pyxides**, the **Tomb of the Balsamario**, **Tomb of the Pyriform Aryballos** which can be dated to between the middle of the 7th and the beginning of the 6th century B.C. Not far off is the

Tomb of the Bronzetto di Offerente (late 6th cent. B.C.) an aedicula tomb, with a gabled roof. It was surrounded by a series of sarcophagi in the open air, which had already been plundered in antiquity, as is the case with most of the other tombs, and which date to the 5th century B.C. On the **Poggio della Porcareccia**, between the slopes of the town and S. Cerbone, are the **Tomb of the Oreficerie** (Goldwork), with personal ornaments in gold and silver, and the **Tomb of the Flabelli**, discovered intact, with jewellery, three magnificent fans in repousse bronze, arms, helmets and a large quantity of bronze receptacles as well as Greek and local pottery. A building was excavated near these tombs. It had several rooms and may have been a center for the industrial processing of metal, active from the end of the 6th century B.C. to late Etruscan times. Unfortunately a lack of evidence makes it impossible to define the precise location and extension of *Pupluna* in its earliest phase, but presumably the built-up area was situated where the town and castle now stand. **City walls** about 2.500 meters long defended the town and a few stretches

114

built with large squared blocks can still be seen. These date to the archaic phase (6th-5th cent. B.C.) when *Pupluna* had become a real city, rich and powerful.

TALAMONE

Once an Etruscan city, then a simple fishing village, the town is now a flourishing seaside resort. The houses are huddled together on a promontory which dominates the sea. Of particular interest is the 16th-century **Rocca** or Fortress which was probably built on a project of Vecchietta, and the remains of the **Etruscan temple** of Talamonaccio. Mention of the town is made in history books, for in 1860 Garibaldi and his Thousand stopped here to replenish themselves with arms before leaving for Marsala.

ROSELLE

The excavations of the Etruscan and Roman city of Roselle can be visited. They lie only a few kilometers from Grosseto. The town, set on two low hills divided by a valley, is surrounded by a **circuit of walls** over three km. long which has been miraculously preserved in its entirety from the 6th century B.C. up to now. Various entrance gates along the wall provide acccess to the city and entrance to the excavations is through the **East Gate**. The road leads to the heart of the Roman city, then to the **Forum**, with broad streets in volcanic stone, on either side of which are the most important public buildings such as the **Basilica**, with a rectangular ground

Above: sarcophagus with figure of the deceased and a female demon from Chianciano. Facing page: general view of the excavations of Roselle.

plan and portico, used for the administration of justice. The paving in stone slabs of the Forum of Imperial times still exists across the way. Further south is what is thought to have been the seat of the *Augustales*, a room with niches in the walls, which contained the marble statues of the emperor Claudius, Livia and other personages of the Julio-Claudian dynasty, evidence of the cult of the imperial family. Protected by modern shed roofs, the remains of various **Etruscan houses** from the archaic period (one with two rooms, one with a circular enclosure, etc.) can be seen under the Roman level. Portions of the walls and floors in pressed clay dating to the 7th-6th century B.C. are still extant. On the slopes of the north hill, not far from the road that leads to the excavations, is a **Roman bath establishment** with mosaic pavements and the base of a **medieval tower**, while near the top of the hill are other **Etruscan buildings** of the archaic period and the **Roman amphitheater** of the 1st century A.D. with four entrances corresponding to the four cardinal points. On the south hill, excavation has brought to light a vast **inhabited center** with streets, houses and artisan workshops of the late 6th century B.C., over which lies a later urban settlement of the Hellenistic period.

For a clear correct interpretation of the excavations of the city and of the necropolises, the artistic production and the economy of Roselle, one would do well to visit the permanent exhibition, installed on scientific bases, in the Museo Archeologico of Grosseto.

Above, left: boats near the Argentario; right: the town of Orbetello. Facing page, below: a view of the Laguna of Orbetello.

ORBETELLO

The town is at the center of the lagoon of Orbetello, which is about 27 kilometers square, with two strips of sand known as *tomboli*. An artificial dam, built in 1842, joins it to the promontory of the Argentario. A visit to Orbetello can begin with the **Porta Medina Coeli**, which was part of the old circuit of walls. The gate leads into the Piazza Quattro Novembre, surrounded by the **Spanish fortifications** from the period when it was part of the Spanish garrisons: these fine examples of military architecture were begun by Philip II and continued by Philip III in the 17th century. The 14th-century **Cathedral** is also lovely, although it was remodelled in the 17th century. Inside is a fine marble *altarpiece* of pre-Romanesque art.

The Palazzo della Pretura houses the **Antiquarium**, a museum with archaeological material from Etruscan and Roman times from all over the city territory. Particular attention should be paid to the archaic *sphinx* of the 7th-6th century B.C., various amphoras and sculpture of fine execution.

ARGENTARIO

This large promontory stretches twelve kilometers out into the sea. It was once an island and then was joined to the continent as sand accumulated to form an isthmus. After this, two stretches of sand joined the isthmus to the mainland, creating the Laguna of Orbetello. On the north this magnifient stretch of land which juts out into the sea slopes down into a lovely bay in which Porto Santo Stefano is situated. Tourist villages have sprung up everywhere in the past years.

Above: the old fortification of Porto Ercole. Facing page, above: the berthing place of Porto Santo Stefano; below: a view of the town.

PORTO ERCOLE

This picturesque coastal town and seaside resort lies on the east coast of the Argentario. The old part of the town clusters around charming streets and small squares where various fine buildings are to be noted: the estimable **Palazzo Consani** (once seat of the Spanish governor), the **Parish Church**, in which Caravaggio was buried; the spacious **Villa Corsini** with a lovely park that is almost a botanical garden with a wealth of rare plants. Dominating the houses from up high is the large complex of the **Rocca** with the forts of **Santa Barbara**, **Monte Filippo** and **Stella**, all built by the Spaniards.

PORTO SANTO STEFANO

This well known seaside resort was almost entirely destroyed in World War II and has been fully rebuilt. Now a flourishing port (with the Porto Vecchio and the Porto Nuovo) it has a large fishing fleet. In the town itself note should be taken of the **Church of Santo Stefano**, built in the 17th century but completely reconstructed after the war, and, above the town, the old bare Rocca or fortress. The small picturesque streets are the chief attraction of this pleasant tranquil town.

Above: the nucleus of Giglio Castello. Facing page: the bay of Giglio Porto.

ISOLA DEL GIGLIO

Once occupied by the Etruscans as documented by the remains of a ship that was wrecked in the waters of Giglio Porte, the **Villa of the Enobarbi** in località Castellari, however, dates to Roman times. Reconstructions and hypotheses advanced by historians and based on what remains would seem to indicate that the villa had rooms with barrel vaults, decorated with marble and varicolored stuccoes and with a complex system of piping which carried running water to various rooms. There was a *cetaria*, or a fish pond, next to the building. Other remains of Roman buildings have been found near Giglio Castello. In 1362 the island of Giglio passed from the Pisans to the Genoese and after various vicissitudes became a Florentine possession.

The brief journey from Giglio Porto to Giglio Castello (about six km.) is one of the most fascinating experiences available to a tourist in the entire Tuscan archipelago. From **Giglio Porto**, a small center clustered around its bay, the road rises steeply in the midst of terraced vineyards to the imposing **Torre del Lazzeretto** and further on the **Faro Vecchio**. After a series of curves the austere brooding town of **Giglio Castello** appears ahead, completely enclosed in the grey medieval walls with their cylindrical and rectangular towers, and at the summit the 14th-century **Fortress**. Even if the entire town of Giglio Castello can be considered, in its homogeneity, as a single work of art, particular note should be taken of the **Parish Church** which has been restored but which still reveals its 14th-century origins. The asphalt road which joins Giglio Porto to Giglio Castello has a single fork which leads to **Campese**, a tiny village which is the paradise of scuba divers thanks to its limpid water and the variety of fish. Next to the village is the **Torre del Campese** built during the reign of Francesco I, grand duke of Tuscany.

Above: a view of the springs of the spa at Saturnia. Facing page: Sorano (above) and Pitigliano, ancient centers of Etruscan origin clinging to steep tufa spurs.

SATURNIA

This small town lies surrounded by the circuit of walls built by the Sienese in 1461 on what was left of the preceding walls thought to be Etruscan. It is known mostly for the **springs** of sulphurous water (37.5°) useful in curing ailments of the respiratory system and in rheumatology. A visit to the **Etruscan necropolis** a few kilometers from the inhabited center is quite interesting. There are numerous tombs in slabs of travertine.

SORANO

The town is of Etruscan origin, not surprising in an area densely settled by the Etruscans. In the vicinity is the **Etruscan necropolis of Sovana**, excavated at the beginning of the century, with numerous chamber tombs dating to the 4th-3rd century B.C. They are cut into the tufa walls of the cliff that was created by the Calesina and its affluents. The most interesting is perhaps the **Tomba Ildebranda**, of the 2nd century B.C., in the shape of a temple with columns, and capitals in the shape of a temple with columns, and capitals in the form of human heads. But the Sorano we see now is that of the Middle Ages, when it belonged to the Aldobrandeschi and then to the Orsini, before becoming part of the Medici grand duchy. The main square contains the **Parish church**, remodelled in the 18th century. The **Rocca degli Orsini** or fortress, built in the 15th century and later enlarged, is also imposing. The coats of arms of the Aldobrandeschi and the Orsini recall times past. This is the place from which to get a vast panorama.

PITIGLIANO

Originally an important Etruscan, and later, Roman city, it now has a historical center of characteristically medieval origins. Particularly striking is the **Cathedral** with a fine Baroque facade and numerous important works inside. Also worthy of note is the 14th-century **Palazzo Orsini**, modified in the 16th century by Giuliano da Sangallo, and the simple **Church of Santa Maria** with a late Renaissance facade and a tripartite interior with various fine works of art.

THE AMIATA

The Amiata is the highest mountain peak in Tuscany (1738 m.) and is quite outstanding from a naturalistic point of view. The mountain is of volcanic origin and dates to the Quaternary period. Small streams and springs abound and in recent decades it has become a winter sport station with elaborate ski facilities and refuges and ski runs. The Amiata also is fairly well populated with towns such as **Abbadia San Salvatore, Piancastagnaio, Santa Fiora, Arcidosso, Castel del Piano** which contain buildings which bear witness to the past and which are well known for their beauty.

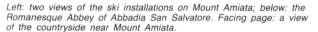

Left: two views of the ski installations on Mount Amiata; below: the Romanesque Abbey of Abbadia San Salvatore. Facing page: a view of the countryside near Mount Amiata.

SIENA

On the softly rolling hills of the countryside between the valleys of the Arbia, the Elsa and the Merse lies Siena. This city with its medieval imprint can be seen in all its sober austere beauty as it unravels through alleys, small streets, closed-in suburbs, airy squares. It is truly one of the finest examples of a medieval city. Various sporadic finds testify that the area now occupied by the city was already inhabited in the bronze age. An Etruscan settlement also seems to have been established on the site of the current town. But the first detailed information dates to Roman times. We, know, for instance, that Siena, at the time *Sena Julia*, must have been a Roman *civitas*, founded as a military colony by Caesar (a legend maintains that the city was founded by Aschio and Senio, Remo's two sons). In the Lombard period Siena was already quite famous. After the Carolingian conquest it was subject to the pre-eminence of the Bishops until the 11th century when it became a free commune. This was when the city experienced its first great period of territorial and urban expansion, thanks to the flourishing commerce and trade which depended on the route followed by the Via Francigena which put the city in communication with the area north of the Alps. In the 12th and 13th centuries the city, by now rich and powerful (Sienese bankers used to lend considerable sums to sovereigns, popes and princes), often clashed with the neighboring city of Florence on which it inflicted a crushing defeat in 1260 in the famous battle of Monteaperti. These were also the years in which some of the most important trends in medieval painting took form in Siena. Outstanding personalities such as Duccio da Buoninsegna, Simone Martini, Ambrogio Lorenzetti came into the world and left inimitable masterpieces, influencing with their works all of 14th-century art. In 1269 the Sienese were this time drastically defeated at Colle Val d'Elsa by the Florentine troops. It meant the beginning of a decline which, with its ups and downs, intensified in the course of the following centuries. In fact in 1487 Siena became a signoria under the aegis of Pandolfo Petrucci. In the 16th century it allied itself with Charles V and then with Philip II and in 1559 surrendered to the troops of Giangiacomo de' Medici and passed under the dominion of Cosimo I. In the centuries that followed it fell under the Lorraine, following the sorts of the Grand Duchy of Tuscany. In 1859 it was the first Tuscan city annexed to the Kingdom of Italy.

At the side: a view of Siena with the Palazzo Pubblico and the Piazza del Campo at the center.

PIAZZA DEL CAMPO AND PALAZZO PUBBLICO

Piazza del Campo, one of the most distinctive squares in Italy, gives the impression of a stage set as it slopes down towards the Palazzo Pubblico in a sort of bowl shape. Most of it is paved in brick and the elegant **Fonte Gaia** stands at the center of the hemicycle. The lovely reliefs by Jacopo della Quercia, which once decorated the fountain, are now in the Palazzo Pubblico and reproductions have taken their place on the fountain. The **Palazzo Pubblico**, built between the 13th and the 14th century, may well be the most elegant civic building in Italy. The facade consists of a central section (the oldest part) and two perfectly symmetrical slightly lower wings. The lower part of the complex is in stone and the upper part in brick, all enhanced by fine rows of three-light windows. The interior is a real treasure chest of peerless masterpieces: the rooms on the ground floor (now Town Hall) contain important *frescoes* by Vecchietta, Simone Martini, Sano di Pietro and Sodoma.

Above: the Piazza del Campo and the Palazzo Pubblico with the Torre del Mangia. Facing page, above: the Fonte Gaia, and, below, the fresco of Guidoriccio da Fogliano, by Simone Martini, inside the Palazzo Pubblico.

On the first floor one can visit the important **Museo Civico** which has one of the finest art collections in Tuscany. The museum itinerary winds through various rooms, all of which are almost completely covered with frescoes. Works by Spinello Aretino, Parri di Spinello, Jacopo della Quercia, Taddeo di Bartolo, Sodoma, Simone Martini, Vecchietta, and Sano di Pietro can be admired. Two frescoes by Simone Martini, the *Maestà* and *Guidoriccio da Fogliano*, both dating to the first half of the 14th century, are in the **Sala del Mappamondo**. The top floor houses Etruscan material from the excavations of Murlo.

CATHEDRAL

Dedicated to the Virgin of the Assumption, it is certainly built on the site of a precedent church. Construction began towards the end of the 12th century and in the

Above, and facing page: two views of the imposing structure of the Cathedral of Siena.

third decade of the 13th century there is unmistakeable mention of the *Opera di Santa Maria*. Work on the Cathedral continued throughout the 13th century. A little after the middle of the century the dome and the first apse of the building were finished, but they were torn down in the second decade of the 14th century when Camaino di Crescentino, father of Tino, began the elongation of the apse towards Vallepiatta. In the meanwhile around 1290 Giovanni Pisano had built the lower part of the facade. But before the middle of the 14th century work on the Cathedral came to a halt because the economic and demographic growth of the city, together perhaps with the desire to emulate the great cathedral of its rival Florence, induced the Sienese to plan a church of such a size that the existing building would have served as transept. Lando di Pietro began the construction in 1339, then continued by Giovanni di Agostino and by Domenico di Agostino. But either due to errors in calculations of a static nature, or the change in the economic and political situation, as well as the plague of the middle of the century, the ambitious project was abandoned in 1355. The **bell tower** is also Romanesque in structure, although lightened by the two-color marble facing. It seems to have been built on a precedent tower of the Bisdomini and is pierced by a series of openings

that shift from one-light to six-light as they rise, and is topped by an octagonal base pyramid. The Cathedral of Siena encloses an incredible number of works of art, which together with those preserved in the adjacent **Museo dell'Opera** provide a complete survey of the artistic culture at its zenith. Obviously only the most important can be touched on: on the **facade** mention must be made of Giovanni Pisano's *statues*, executed around 1290. **Inside** the first thing to take into consideration is the marble *pavement*, decorated in sgraffiti or intarsia subdivided into about fifty panels carried out between the middle of the 14th and the middle of the 16th century. A score or so of artists, mostly Sienese, including Domenico di Niccolò and Domenico Beccafumi, had a hand in the work. The *high altar* in the presbytery is by Baldassarre Peruzzi, with the large *ciborium* by Vecchietta; two of the *angels* are by Francesco di Giorgio Martini and others are by Beccafumi. In the left transept, near the area covered by the dome, is the famous octagonal *pulpit* by Nicola Pisano with *Events from the Life of Christ* in the parapet, the scenes separated from

Facing page: the two-color interior of the Cathedral. Above: the interior of the Piccolomini Library, a late 15th-century building which contains precious frescoes by Pinturicchio.

each other by *prophets* and *angels*. Executed with the help of Nicola's son Giovanni, Arnolfo di Cambio, Donato and Lapo di Ricevuto, it must be considered as one of the basic stages in Gothic sculpture. In the centuries that followed, the Sienese continued to focus their attention on the Cathedral, as shown by the addition of numerous chapels. Mention must be made of the **Chapel of San Ansano** with the *monument to Cardinal Petroni* by Tino di Camaino and the *tomb slab* of Bishop Giovanni Pecci, a bronze by Donatello. The **Chapel of**

St. John the Baptist is a Renaissance structure by Giovanni di Stefano, with a bronze *Baptist* by Donatello and *frescoes* by Pinturicchio. The **Chapel of the Sacrament** is also rich in works of art, while the **Chapel of the Madonna del Voto** (or «*Chigi Chapel*») was sponsored by Alexander VII shortly after the middle of the 17th century, with the plan by Bernini. To the right of the Cathedral stands what remains of the **Duomo Nuovo**, including the facade, the portal on the right side which leads to the Sabatelli stairs, while in the right aisle the rooms for the **Museo dell'Opera Metropolitana** were obtained by closing off the first three arches.

135

CHURCH OF SANTA MARIA DI PROVENZANO

The church, built in 1594 by Flaminio del Turco on a design by the Carthusian Damiano Schifardini has a single nave with a transept and a dome that rises up on an octagonal drum over the crossing. Many 16th-century works of art are preserved **inside** (Manetti, Vanni, Casolani) as well as the venerated *Madonna di Provenzano*.

SANCTUARY OF SANTA CATERINA

The complex developed around the saint's house which was transformed into a sanctuary in 1464. First comes the **Oratorio Superiore** (Upper Oratory) with many fine paintings. A small loggia attributed to Baldassarre Peruzzi leads to the **Oratory of the Crucifix**, entirely lined with frescoes, most of which are by Giuseppe Nasini. Turning right at the entrance to the sanctuary the path leads to the so-called **Oratorio della Camera** and the small **cell** where the Saint spent most of her time and where objects which belonged to her are still kept. A small door on the lower floor leads into the **Church of Santa Caterina in Fontebranda**, known also as *Oratorio della Contrada*.

Left: the Church of Santa Maria di Provenzano; below: the Sanctuary of Santa Caterina.

CHURCH OF SAN DOMENICO

It was begun in the first half of the 13th century and building continued throughout the 14th century to be finally finished after the middle of the 15th century. Since the land on which the church is built slopes sharply down, the large crypt has been installed under the back, as in the church of San Francesco. The **crypt** is divided into a nave and two aisles by robust piers which support the cross vaults. To the right of the church is the 15th-century **Cloister**. Mention inside should be made of the *frescoes* by Sodoma in the **Chapel of Saint Catherine**; the *ciborium* and the *angels* on the high altar by Benedetto da Maiano; a detached *fresco* by Pietro Lorenzetti; and then works by Matteo di Giovanni, Vanni, Francesco di Giorgio Martini, Sodoma, Casolani, Sano di Pietro, Manetti, while some of the *stained-glass windows* are by modern or contemporary artists.

FONTEBRANDA

In the 13th century was installed the fountain **Fontebranda**, which was not only an outstanding example of Gothic architecture, but which constituted the visible part of a complex daring subterranean network of acqueducts.

Right: the Church of San Domenico; below: the construction of Fontebranda.

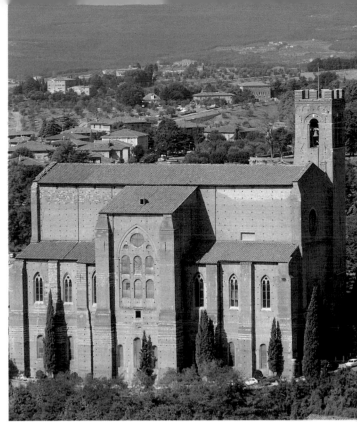

Above and facing page: various stages of the Palio and the procession in costume.

THE PALIO

While the Palio of Siena can also be thought of as a holi-day, it is first and foremost a yearly occasion to renew the rivalries between the districts into which the city is divided, a means of giving free reign to the age-old hostility between one district and the other; hostility which vanishes as if by magic once the race has been run, to return the moment the next Palio comes round. Every year the Palio takes place in the Piazza del Campo on July 2nd and on August 16th. All in all 17 districts are involved, each of them named after a real or imagi-nary animal: Aquila (eagle), Chiocciola (snail), Onda (wave), Panther (panther), Selva (rhinocerous and oak), Tartuca (tortoise), Civetta (owl), Leocorno (unicorn), Nicchio (ocean shell), Torre (elephant with tower), Val-dimontone (rampant ram), Bruco (caterpillar), Drago (dragon), Giraffa, Istrice (porcupine), Lupa (wolf), Oca (goose) and each one is represented by participants who parade through the Piazza del Campo in splendid Rei-nassance costumes before the beginning of each race. In its present form the race dates back to the first half of the 15th century, even though a less characteristic ver-sion was run in Siena as early as the 13th century.

The procession which takes place before the Palio is par-ticularly striking: one after the other, mace-bearers, the standard bearer of the Commune, the trumpeteers and palace musicians, the representatives of the five captains, of the 13 districts governed by the podestà and the 18 vicariates which, in olden times, constituted the Republic of Siena; then comes the Capitano del Popolo on horse-back, followed by the participants of the ten districts which will take part in the race (for every race seven dis-tricts are excluded by drawing lots), and finally the wag-on which carries the Palio or banner, which is the prize for the winning district. At the tail end of the procession come the ten horses and the jockeys who will vie in the race. The horses are lined up near a rope, known as "*canapo*" and when it is lowered they streak off to circle the piazza three times. The course is almost circular and downhill in stretches and anything but easy for the horses and their riders, but the prize at stake is high and at the end the winner will be carried in triumph and celebrated for days on end.

Above: a view of the town center of Monteriggioni; below: the Porta Volterrana in Colle di Val d'Elsa.

MONTERIGGIONI

The village of Monteriggioni clings to a small hillside, enclosed in the impressive circuit of **walls**. From a distance the first impression as we glance from one four-sided **tower** to the other (there are all of fourteen set along the walls) is that time has stood still and we are still in the Middle Ages. The village was built in 1203 by the Sienese who used it as an outpost against the Florentines and as a result of its critical site it often changed hands. The walls went up between 1213 and 1219 and extend for about 570 meters, encircling the tiny but compact charming village which has a fine **Parish Church** built in a transitional Romanesque-Gothic style.

COLLE DI VAL D'ELSA

Situated at the center of an area that was already settled in Etruscan and Roman times, Colle was an independent commune in the 13th century even though it was allied

The haunting interior of the Abbey of San Galgano.

to Florence. In the middle of the 14th century it passed under the domination of Florence and as Siena declined Colle experienced a period of peace and economical prosperity based on industrial installations which exploited the hydraulic energy of the Elsa river. The urban structure of the historical center of Colle consists of an upper part (**Colle Alto**) and a part that began to develop on the plain in the Middle Ages (**Colle Basso**). The upper part obviously mirrors the lay of the land and stretches out along the ridge of the hill, divided into the clearly separate parts of **Castello** and **Borgo**.

ABBEY OF SAN GALGANO

This complex of buildings was one of the most important for the diffusion of the Gothic-Cistercian style in Italy. The **Church** is a Latin cross and is faced with travertine and brick. It was built by the Cistercian monks between 1224 and 1238. Its slow decline began in the 16th century and restoration was required as early as 1577. In the 18th century the church was partially destroyed when the campanile and some of the vaults collapsed. The incompleted facade has four columns and three round-headed arches with ogive extrados. The side walls contain lovely one-light openings, some of which are surmounted by an oculus, as well as the same number of fine ogive two-light openings. The apse has two tiers of one-light windows. Grass now grows over the vast interior which has been roofless for decades. The nave and two aisles have sixteen cruciform piers with four semi-engaged columns. The lovely arches are Gothic with double archivolts. The vaulting of the nave has disappeared. The transept, which is still well preserved, has three aisles with the one on the east transformed into four small chapels. Next to the church is the **Monastery** but nothing is left but the *Chapter Hall* and the *Monks' Hall* with two aisles and piers. On the upper floor a narrow corridor leads to the monks' cells and the choir.

Above: a view of the old town of San Gimignano. Facing page: the Salvucci towers inside the town.

SAN GIMIGNANO

The architecture of San Gimignano makes this small city, so concentrated and noble, unique with the geometric pattern of the towers rising above the town. It was already known in Etruscan and Roman times. During the Middle Ages its importance grew thanks to the presence of the Via Francigena, the most important route at the time which connected Italy to all of Europe. San Gimignano almost always sided with Florence, but was unable to expand its power or its boundaries further because geographically it was inhibited by nearby Florence and Siena.

The two urban spaces with the greatest wealth, artistically speaking, are the **Piazza della Cisterna** and the Piazza Duomo. The former takes its name from the 13th-century cistern set almost in the center of the square. All around is a series of medieval buildings including, on the south, the **Palazzo Tortolini Treccani** (14th cent.) with two tiers of two-light windows, the **Casa Salvestrini** and the **Casa Razzi** (13th cent.); on the west side, the twin **Guelph Towers** of the Ardinghelli (13th cent.); and lastly, on the north, the **Palazzo Cortesi** flanked by the **tower** of the same name known also as Torre del Diavolo (Devil's Tower).

The **Palazzo del Podestà**, built in 1239 and enlarged about a century later, rises up on the **Piazza Duomo**. There is a fine *fresco* by Sodoma on the ground floor. One of the tallest towers (51 m.), the **Torre known as Rognosa**, rises up over the palace, while right across the way is the **Collegiata**, built around 1239 on the ruins of the old parish church of San Gimignano, with a fine facade in brick and stone. The tripartite Romanesque interior has magnificent cross vaulting. On the internal wall of the facade there are *frescoes* by Taddeo di Bartolo, and, at the sides, two *wooden statues* by Jacopo della Quercia (1421). The walls are entirely covered with fine frescoes: on the wall of the right aisle there is a beautiful cycle depicting *Scenes and Episodes of the*

New Testament by Barna da Siena. At the back of the aisle is the **Chapel of Santa Fina** (patron saint of the city), with terra cottas by Giuliano and Benedetto da Maiano; the frescoes on the side walls with *Episodes from the Life of the Saint* are by Ghirlandaio (1475), the fine *altar piece* is by Giuliano da Maiano. On the wall of the left aisle there is another fresco cycle of *Stories of the Old Testament*. Note the fine *ciborium* (1475) by Benedetto da Maiano on the high altar and an *Annunciation* by Ghirlandaio in the loggia of the *Baptistery*. The **Palazzo del Popolo** (now Town Hall) stands to the left of the Collegiata. It was built in the second half of the 13th century and enlarged in the early decades of the next century. The fine facade is spangled with the coats of arms of the podestà. Inside are the **Museo Civico** and the **Pinacoteca Civica**. The former is installed on the top floor and exhibits extremely interesting works including a fresco of the *Maestà* by Lippo Memmi. The latter contains a valuable collection of paintings of the schools of Siena and Florence from the 13th to the 15th

centuries, including works by Filippino Lippi, Coppo di Marcovaldo, Pinturicchio and Benozzo Gozzoli. Near the Piazza del Duomo is the **Piazza Pecori** with the fine **Palazzo della Propositura**, seat of the **Museum of Religious Art** with its rich collection of paintings, precious church furnishings and minor arts. Near the square is the **Rocca**, built by the Florentines in 1353. This solid bastion is pentagonal in plan and has small towers and the remains of walls. Other historical buildings of note include the **Church of San Bartolomeo** (13th cent.), with a brick facade decorated with two orders of blind arches; the **Church of Sant'Agostino** (late 13th cent.), with an extremely simple facade and works by Benozzo Gozzoli, Lippo Memmi and Bartolo di Fredi inside; the **Church of San Pietro** (11th cent.); the **Church of San Jacopo** (13th cent.), with a nave only and unusual elements in the vaults which spring from transverse arches on engaged piers with half columns; and finally the former **Church of San Francesco** (now used as a wine cellar) with a lovely white facade.

143

Above: the courtyard of the Town Hall with the typical covered staircase; left: one of the streets of the town. Facing page: the Piazza della Cisterna, surrounded by towers
and with the water reservoir from which it takes its name
at the center.

Facing page: abstract patterns of rows of grape vines near a farm in the Chianti district. Above: the town of Radda in Chianti.

THE CHIANTI

The region of the Chianti with its gentle hilly contryside is bordered by the basin of the Arno to the south of Florence and that of the Ombrone, north of Siena. The area was already inhabited in the time of the Etruscans and then passed under Roman rule. In the 8th century it became a large feud of the noble Firidolfi family. It afterwards became the object of conquest and contention between Siena and Arezzo first, and later between Siena and Florence. The landscape the Chianti presents its visitors is rich in a hundred different ways: it is rich in roads, unpaved country lanes which retain their charm of long ago, steep paths that wind up to a villa or a castle, parish church or farm. The Chianti is a "holy" land (small churches everywhere with an age-old history) and a land of towers, rich in castles (they can be counted by the dozen) where the atmosphere is still authentically medieval. The most important are **Castellina**, with fine fortifications and old palaces; **Radda**, with its 15th-century Palazzo Pretorio; and **Greve**, with its unique main square.

It is hardly necessary to say that the principal activity in the region of the Chianti is agriculture: an agriculture which produces wine famous in every nook and corner of the world, the "Chianti Classico Gallo Nero", and an olive oil that is just as prized and which is to be found on the tables of true gourmets. The territory of the Chianti is formed of lias limestone (*alberese*), sandstone (*macigno*), clay schist (*galestro*). Over half of the territory is covered by tall trees: oaks, chestnuts, ilex (holm-oak), firs and in part by the so-called Mediterranean

Above: the Farm of Montemaggio, where the fine Chianti classico wines are produced; at the side: vineyards in the heart of the Chianti. Facing page: the Badia at Coltibuono built around the year Thousand.

scrub including shrubs, brambles, bushes, hedges, aromatic plants. The other half of the land is cultivated as farmland: large vineyards which cover the hillsides in geometric patterns, extensive olive groves that stretch to the horizon. The wine of this land, known for centuries for its delicious aroma, is the result of a perfect mixture of four types of grapes: Sangioveto and canaiolo (purple grapes), malvasia and trebbiano (white grapes). The result is Chianti Classico, a ruby-red wine, with a full dry flavor, with just the right amount of tannic acid and the characteristic perfume of violets, the masterpiece of this generous land which has managed to keep its "flavor" of times past.

On this page: the town halls of Montepulciano (above, left), of Pienza (above) and of Montalcino (left).

MONTEPULCIANO

The town was already in existance in Etruscan times, and is still medieval and Renaissance in appearance. The **Cathedral** was built between 1592 and 1630 and contains a *Madonna and Child* by Sano di Pietro and various terra cottas by the Della Robbias.

The **Church of S. Agostino** is by Michelozzo and the 14th-century church of Sant'Agostino contains a fine 13th-century *crucifix*. In addition to the **Palazzo Comunale** the **Palazzo Neri Orselli** merits mention. Inside is the Museo Civico with a collection of prestigious paintings and sculpture.

PIENZA

Pienza is an authentic masterpiece of town planning. It is the ideal model of a large Renaissance city whose development did not depend on the ups and downs of history. All the basic elements of a much larger city are present in this town which owes its origins to Pope Pius II Piccolomini: from the central square to the buildings which surround it - the Cathedral, the Bishop's Palace, the Patrician Palace and the Town Hall.

The **Cathedral** was built between 1459 and 1462 on a project by Rossellino. The fine facade in travertine has three portals separated by pilasters flanked by two orders of columns. The luminous interior has a nave and two aisles and contains works by great artists including

A view of Chianciano.

Giovanni di Paolo, Matteo di Giovanni, Vecchietta, Sano di Pietro and Rossellino himself.

To the left of the Cathedral is the old **Canons' House** which houses the **Cathedral Museum** with paintings of the Sienese school, goldsmiths' work, illuminated 15th- and 16th-century chorales. The fine **Bishop's Palace** rises up next to it with a lovely facade with two tiers of Guelph-cross windows. The **Town Hall** stands across from the Cathedral. It was rather thoroughly restructured after 1900 and is in travertine with an austere portal above which are four two-light windows. Lastly, to the right of the Cathedral is the splendid **Palazzo Piccolomini**, also by Rossellino and clearly inspired by the Rucellai Palace in Florence. The square building, built in rusticated ashlar, has a facade that is articulated by fine two-light windows. The interior, which can be visited, has many rooms which contain important works of art. The courtyard and the hanging gardens (one of the finest examples of the kind) are also particularly lovely.

MONTALCINO

This small medieval city stands high up on top of an upland between the valleys of the Ombrone and the Asso Rivers. Both Florence and Siena laid claims to the city and eventually it landed up in the Medici sphere of influence in 1555. The economy centers around the production of "Brunello di Montalcino", a very fine wine for which the city is famous throughout the world.

Of the many buildings in the historical center which testify to its past, mention must be made of the **Cathedral**, a large structure that was completely rebuilt at the beginning of the 19th century; the **Church of S. Egidio** (14th cent.) which contains a fine fresco of the 15th-century Sienese school; the **Church of Sant'Agostino** (14th cent.) with a simple gabled facade and with various Sienese frescoes dating to the 14th century inside; the **Church of San Francesco** (13th cent.); the imposing **Palazzo Comunale** (town hall) (13th-14th cent.); the **Museo Diocesano** (installed inside the Seminary) which boasts of a valuable collection, consisting above all of works by Sienese artists of the 14th and 15th centuries. The **Museo Civico** contains outstanding works by 14th- and 15th-century Tuscan artists. The **Museo Archeologico** houses prehistoric and Etruscan archaeological material found in the area; and lastly, not to be overlooked, is the beautiful **Rocca** or Fortress, built in 1361.

CHIANCIANO

The Etruscans were already acquainted with Chianciano, one of the best known spas in Italy. The waters are particularly effective in curing liver ailments. Remains of the circuit of **walls**, as well as of the **Fortress**, can still be seen in the city; note should also be taken of the **Collegiata of S. Giovanni Battista**, the **Palazzo del Podestà**, the **Palazzo dell'Arcipretura**, seat of the **Museo d'Arte Sacra**.

AREZZO

Arezzo is the furthest inland of the Tuscan cities, surrounded by small mountain ranges. It is situated at the confluence of four fertile valleys: the Casentino, the Valdichiana, the upper Valdarno, and the upper part of the Valtiberina.

The area already seems to have been inhabited in Villanovan times, but it was not until the Etruscans came that Arezzo rapidly became a flourishing powerful center. Together with Volterra, Roselle, Vetulonia and Chiusi it was one of the most important Etruscan cities of the time, and even promised aid to the Latins against the king of Rome, Tarquinius Priscus. In the 5th century it was already a large *lucumony* and in the centuries immediately thereafter it became one of the most important cities in Italy after Rome. Under Roman domination it continued to prosper until the 1st-2nd century A.D. when as a result of incurable internecine struggles it rapidly declined. In 575 it fell under Lombard rule and then passed to the Franks until it became part of the Marchesate of Tuscany. In the 11th century it became a free commune, in a period characterized by renewed vigor and an increase in building activity. The city contested Florentine supremacy over the region until it was finally irremediably defeated by Florence in the battle of Campaldino (1289). Arezzo thus fell under the Florentine sphere of influence, together with so many other cities, then part of the Grand Duchy of Tuscany under the Medicis and then under the Lorrainers. The center of the city lies on the slope of a hill. Above, dominating the urban fabric, is the **Piazza del Duomo**, above which rises the **Cathedral**, begun in 1227 in Gothic form. The facade was rebuilt in the early 20th century. Tall piers supporting cross vaulting separate the side aisles from the nave. There is no transept. Magnificent *stained-glass windows* by Guillaume de Marcillat flood the interior with light. In addition the church contains the 14th-century **Cappella Tarlati** and in the left aisle near the Sacristy a beautiful fresco of the *Magdalen* by Piero della Francesca. Important works dating from the 14th to the 17th century are on exhibition in the adjacent **Museo Diocesano**. Near the square is the imposing structure of the **Medici Fortress**, rebuilt in the

16th century by Antonio da Sangallo. This robust star-shaped fortification with bastions is characterized by the high escarpment on top of which is a short stretch of wall. Nearby is the **Piazza Grande**, the most picturesque and monumental corner of the city. Buildings dating to the 14th, 15th and 16th centuries face onto the square. The most noteworthy include the fine **Palazzo della Fraternità dei Laici**, a building in Gothic-Renaissance style, designed and for the most part built by Rossellino; the imposing **Palazzo delle Logge** built on designs by Vasari; the medieval **Torre dei Lappoli** and **Torre Faggiolana**. Not far off is the striking **Pieve di Santa Maria** (12th-14th cent.), one of the outstanding Romanesque buildings in the entire region. The marvelous facade was clearly inspired by Pisan-Romanesque precedents. The tripartite interior has a fine trussed timber roof. At the back is the entrance to the austere crypt, which lies under the presbytery. Nearby is the **Palazzo Pretorio** (14th-16th cent.) with a facade completely covered by the coats of arms of the Florentine vicars, and the **House** where **Francesco Petrarca** was born. Of note is the **Palazzo dei Priori** (Town Hall), an austere structure in stone with crenellations and two tiers of windows on the facade. Not to be overlooked are the lovely **Church of San Domenico** (13th-14th cent.), an austere Gothic building with a Romanesque portal, and inside a precious *Crucifix* by Cimabue on the high altar and walls lined with *frescoes* by Spinello Aretino; **Vasari's House**, with frescoes mostly by Vasari; the **Church of the S.S. Annunziata** (15th cent.); the **Church of Badia** (13th cent.); and, above all, the **Church of San Francesco** (13th-14th cent.) which contains Piero della Francesca's marvelous fresco cycle of the *Legend of the True Cross*, one of the greatest works of the entire 15th century. Note should also be taken of the **Galleria e Museo Medievale e Moderno**, where the works of the major Aretine artists from the Middle Ages through the Renaissance are on display, and the **Archaeological Museum** which houses interesting prehistoric, Roman and above all Etruscan material and is situated near the ruins of the **Roman Amphitheater**.

Facing page: a view of the Piazza Grande in Arezzo; right, above: the Town Hall; below: the frescoes by Piero della Francesca inside the Church of San Francesco.

On these two pages: various phases of the Joust of the Saracen, a tournament of medieval origins still held in the Piazza Grande.

GIOSTRA DEL SARACINO

This old tradition dating all the way back to the Middle Ages was not reinstated until 1930. The first Sunday in September the four quarters into which the city is divided participate in this famous joust which takes place in the Piazza Grande. The *Saracino* (a gigantic bust in wood with a steel plaque on his left arm and a long cat-o-nine-tails, to which three leather-covered lead balls are attached, on his right arm) is set up in the north-east corner of the square. Each quarter is represented by a knight who has to strike the plaque with a spear and avoid being hit by the cat-o-nine-tails which in the meantime has begun to spin wildly. It is a difficult game and also rather dangerous for the knight, but the game is enthusiastically cheered by the crowd of Aretines and tourists who come from everywhere to watch.

Above, left: the Town Hall of Cortona; above: the Fort of the Girifalco; left: a panorama of the town and the Val di Chiana seen from the Etruscan walls.

CORTONA

Already famous in Etruscan times, Cortona became an ally of Rome in the 4th century B.C. In the 13th century it became a free commune but at the end of the century it was occupied by Arezzo. After alternating political vicissitudes the city became a signoria of the Casali family. In 1411 it entered the Florentine sphere of influence and then followed the destiny of the Gran Duchy of Tuscany. The important monuments in the city include the **Cathedral** probably built on the remains of the precedent church of Santa Maria. The building with its austere stone facade was designed and realized by the great Giuliano da Sangallo. The tripartite interior was probably also designed by Sangallo even if it was remodelled with a heavy hand in the 18th century. Interesting works of art in the Cathedral include paintings by Cigoli, the school of Signorelli, and by Alessandro Allori.

The **Church of San Francesco** with its simple linear facade and fine portal dates to the first half of the 13th century. The interior contains fine works of art including works by Cigoli, Raffaele Vanni, Pietro da Cortona and Bernardo Radi.

The **Sanctuary of Santa Margherita** dates to 1856. The

The Convent of la Verna.

tripartite interior has various statues of saints on the piers. There is a 13th-century wooden *Crucifix* in the chapel to the right of the presbytery. The earthly remains of Saint Margaret are in a 17th-century silver urn on the high altar.

The **Church of San Domenico**, with its simple ashlar facade and a fine Gothic portal, dates to the early 15th century. The single-nave interior houses outstanding works of art.

The **Palazzo Comunale** is an imposing building dating to the first half of the 13th century. The facade is preceded by a graceful staircase and is surmounted by a solid tower. Inside is the lovely *Sala del Consiglio* with an imposing 16th-century *fireplace*. The **Museo dell'Accademia Etrusca**, in the old **Palazzo Pretorio**, contains an important collection of Etruscan, Roman and Egyptian finds as well as numerous paintings and objects made between the 13th and the 19th centuries. One of the most interesting examples is a large *bronze lamp* of Etruscan make (5th cent. B.C.).

The **Medici Fortress**, also known as the Girifalco Fortress, dominates the city from the top of the hill, It was built in 1556 by Gabrio Serbelloni and is now used for exhibitions and manifestations.

In the environs of Cortona are to be found the **Church of the Madonna del Calcinaio**, a 16th-century structure, the **Tanella di Pitagora**, which was originally an Etruscan hypogeum (perhaps 4th cent. B.C.), and the **Etruscan Tombs of Camucia**.

LA VERNA

This limestone mountain rises up between the Alps of Serra and the Alps of Catenaia in an area that lies between the valleys of the Arno and the Tiber. Countless pilgrimages wend their way to the famous monastery situated here. In 1213 Count Orlando Cattini donated the mountain to Saint Francis who, with his companions, built various huts which later led to the construction of the hermitage. At present the monastery is composed of various buildings: the **Chiesa Maggiore** or **Basilica**, begun in 1348, is a large complex with Della Robbian terra cottas inside, including an *Annunciation* and an *Adoration of the Child*; the small **Church of Santa Maria degli Angeli**, dating to the early 13th century, houses a lovely altarpiece of the *Assumption of the Virgin* by Andrea della Robbia; the **Chapel of the Stigmata** is situated on the rock where Saint Francis received the stigmata. Other buildings include the small **Chapel of San Bonventura**, the **Chapel of Saint Anthony of Padua**, and various **Cloisters**, the whole a marvelous example of sobriety and restraint.

On this page: the town of Poppi. Facing page: the Castle.

POPPI

One of the most famous monuments of the feudal period in Tuscany is to be found in Poppi: the **Castle of the Guidi counts** built in the 13th century. Entrance into the courtyard is across the moat which encircles the castle. The walls of the court are decorated with fine coats of arms of the magistrates and vicars of Florence who took up residence here after the fall of the Guidi when Poppi was annexed by the Florentine republic. A staircase leads to the first floor, used as a **Museum**. The imposing **Library** is of great interest with more than 15,000 volumes, and a wealth of manuscripts and incunabuli. The medieval town lies at the foot of the castle. Of particular note in the town center is the **Church of the Madonna del Morbo**, begun in 1657 and finished about fifty years later and the **Church of San Fedele**, a very old structure dating to 1185-95.

INDEX